A POPULAR
DICTIONARY
OF SIKHISM

W. Owen Cole
and
Piara Singh Sambhi

CURZON
PRESS

First published in 1990
by Curzon Press
St John's Studios, Church Road, Richmond
Surrey, TW9 2QA

© 1990 W. Owen Cole and Piara Singh Sambhi
Reprinted 1996

Printed in Great Britain by
TJ Press (Padstow) Ltd, Padstow, Cornwall

British Library Cataloguing in Publication Data
A catalogue record for this book is available from the British Library

Library of Congress in Publication Data
A catalog record for this book has been requested

ISBN 0-7007-0202-4 (Pbk)

To Lt. Colonel Jagjit Singh Guleria,
poet, man of letters, devout Sikh,
and friend

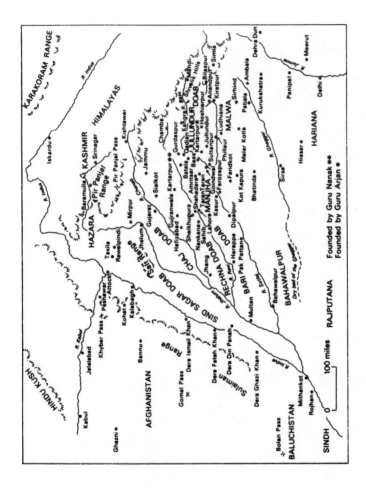

MAP 1 *The Punjab*

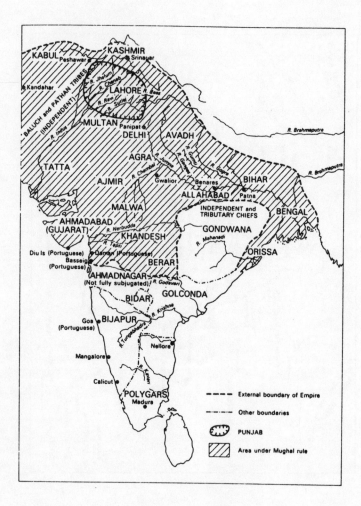

MAP 2 *The Mughal Empire at the death of Akbar (1605)*

INTRODUCTION

The word 'sikh' comes from the Punjabi verb 'sikhna', to learn. A Sikh is therefore a learner, that is, one who learns and follows the path of liberation taught by a man called Gurū Nānak and his nine successors, who lived in the Punjab region of India between 1469 and 1708.

The Sikh religion has only recently come to the academic attention of western scholars. There were a few books written earlier than M. A. Macauliffe's monumental study of the lives and times of the Gurūs, *The Sikh Religion* (Oxford 1909), but these were often the work of soldiers or administrators, like Macauliffe himself, who needed to understand something of the Sikhs for political reasons.

Three views, not necessarily mutually exclusive, tend to have been held of Sikhism by scholars writing during the first half of the twentieth century. One is that Gurū Nānak was a disciple of Kabīr, and that the religion owes its theology largely to him. So G. H. Westcott, *Kabīr and the Kabīr Panth*, Cawnpore, 1907. This interpretation seems to have been accepted by J. N. Farquhar, *Primer of Hinduism*, London, 1912. This book still seems to influence many who write on the period of Indian religion from about the thirteenth century to the death of the last Sikh Gurū in 1708. The source may be indirect, perhaps A. L. Basham, *The Wonder that was India*, Fontana edition, 1971. On page 481 he writes, 'One great religious teacher of modern India, Kabīr (1440 – 1518), a poor weaver of Vārānasī, taught the brotherhood of Hindu and Muslim alike in the fatherhood of God, and opposed idolatry and caste practices, describing that God was equally to be found in temple and mosque. Later, Nānak (1469 – 1539), a teacher of the Punjab, taught the same doctrine with even greater force, and founded a new faith, that of the

9

Sikhs, designed to incorporate all that was best of both Hinduism and Islam.' Here the second view is present, that of Sikhism as a form of deliberate syncretism. It has gained some support among Sikhs themselves eager to portray Gurū Nānak as a forerunner of Māhatmā Gāndhi, a reconciler of Hindu and Muslim. This leads to the third position, the view that Gurū Nānak was a social reformer, seeking to ameliorate the lot of the poor and outcastes of Indian society; again perhaps this idea owes something to the work of Gāndhi.

Examining these interpretations briefly, it is necessary first of all to say that none of them gives any real scope for the insistence found time and again in Gurū Nānak's hymns, that he was being used as a messenger of God. His own words describing his calling will be given later, but meanwhile it is necessary to insist that any interpretation of Sikhism finds a place for the consciousness which the Gurūs had of being instruments of divine revelation. So, to take the third view expressed above first, Sikhism is more than a social reform movement prompted by concern for the plight of men and even more, women, in northern India five hundred years ago. At a time when the Gurūs lacked the political power to bring about social change they were offering spiritual liberation to all, and criticizing forms of religion which were failing to do so either because they regarded some people as beyond the hope of salvation in their present lives, they must be reborn as men and into one of the castes through which liberation could be attained, or because the message which could bring hope was only offering ritualism. Gurū Nānak once said,

> Union with God does not consist of standing outside the huts of ascetics or tombs, going into trances, roaming about, or bathing at pilgrimage places. The way of union is found by dwelling in God while remaining detached in the midst of worldly attachments (Ādi Granth 730).

Gurū Nānak makes many critical remarks about institutional religion and the priests, gurūs, imāms, mullahs and paṇḍits, who make a living from it; he called at least some of them bloodsuckers! 'If a garment is considered polluted and impure with a spot of blood, how can those who suck blood be considered pure?' (AG 140).

Professor Basham's assertion raises a number of issues, two of the more important being the criteria for determining the 'best' in any religion, and whether anyone could hope to produce a synthesis which would satisfy Muslims who, as a primary article of faith accept Muhammad as the seal of the prophets, and can only respect Gurū Nānak as a pīr, a saintly person, or any Hindus for whom ideas of purity and pollution and the institution of caste had any significance. The evidence provided by Gurū Nānak's hymns is that he had no wish to create a religion but wished to enable men and women to experience the truth which lay beyond religions and were often obscured by them. Sikhism itself emerged as a result of circumstances, not intent.

A kinship of ideas with Kabīr cannot be denied, but the evidence of dependence is rejected by those who have studied it carefully (for example, W. H. McLeod 'Kabīr, Nānak, and the Early Sikh Panth', in David N. Lorenzen, *Religious Change and Cultural Domination*, Mexico 1981). Two hagiographies of Gurū Nānak, the *Miharbān* and *Hindālīya janam sākhīs*, describe meetings between the two great teachers at Vārānasī. The *Hindālīya* account which Westcott used is the work of a breakaway movement led by Bidhī Chand, the son of a respected Sikh, Bābā Hindāl. He had no reason to refer favourably to the Gurūs, and may have created a story of Gurū Nānak's acknowledgement of Kabīr as his gurū because of Kabīr's Muslim connections. (Bidhī Chand married a Muslim, his village of Jaṇḍiālā became a centre of opposition to the Gurūs and, in the eighteenth century, the Hindālīs supported the Afghan, Ahmad Shāh Abdālī, against the Khālsā.) The *Miharbān* account has Kabīr saying that Gurū Nānak is a jagat gurū who has come to deliver the world and that Kabīr is his slave! Asked the name of his Gurū, Gurū Nānak replies that it is God.

11

Professor McLeod, in the article already mentioned and some years earlier in *Gurū Nānak and the Sikh Religion*, Oxford, 1968, linked Gurū Nānak with the sant tradition of northern India. Among those associated together by the name 'sant' were Nāmdev, 1270 – 1350, a Mahāhāshtrian calico weaver or tailor, Ravidās (Raidās), an outcaste chamār, leather worker or cobbler, of Vārānasī, and Kabīr himself. The sampradāya, or teaching tradition of the sants, had a number of important elements to it. They were monotheists. They rejected asceticism, celibacy and the worth of outward expressions of religion. They might use names such as 'Rām' in addressing God, but they had no place for sectarian notions whether Hindu or Muslim. It has been said that they regarded the two systems as 'radically wrong and ultimately futile' (ibid. p. 153). The sants taught that spiritual liberation was open to all regardless of caste and sex. Usually they were men of low caste or outcastes, who rejected the authority of brahmins and the *Vedas*, and expressed themselves in what has become known as 'sant bhāṣhā' or 'sadhukkaṛī', a dialect spoken in the Delhi region of North India.

Sikhs have not always been receptive to the inclusion of Gurū Nānak among the sants, because it seems to detract from the individuality or uniqueness of his message, and it could be seen as yet another way of asserting his dependence upon Kabīr. However, this is the group with which he had most in common, and if it can be accepted that the name refers only to a similarity of thought rather than the dependence of any one upon the others there need be no danger of diminishing the distinctive place and role of Gurū Nānak and his successors in the history of Indian religion.

Gurū Nānak was born on 15 April 1469 in a village called Talwaṇḍi, in what is now Pakistan. He was a member of the Bedī zāt, or subgroup, of the Khatrī caste regarded by Sikhs as being of the Kśatria varna of Hinduism. His father was the revenue superintendent of the Muslim owner of the village. The accounts of his life which were written some time after his death, the janam sākhīs, provide a portrait of a child and young man already devout but also sceptical of the ritualism of his parent religion and the status of the brahmins. In an unworldly way he gave money to feed poor beggars when his father told him to put it to good account, and when following his father's occupation he experienced difficulties in counting beyond the number thirteen, tēra, which also meant 'I am yours', and produced a trance-like state of union with God. His marriage was arranged but the birth of two sons did not deflect him from piety. At the age of about thirty Nānak underwent an experience which was to change his life. One morning he took his usual bath in the nearby river but failed to return. Three days later he reappeared but remained silent. When he did eventually speak he said, 'There is neither Hindu nor Muslim so whose path shall I follow? I shall follow God's path. God is neither Hindu nor Muslim, and the path which I follow is God's'. The janam sākhī accounts of this incident have indirect authentication in one of Gurū Nānak's hymns, where he describes himself as an unemployed minstrel who was taken to the divine court, given a robe to show whose servant he was, initiated, commissioned and told what song to sing to the world. It reads,

I was an out of work minstrel, the Lord gave me employment.
The mighty one instructed me, 'Sing my praise night and day'. The Lord summoned me to court, bestowed the robe on me of honouring and praising the Lord.
The Lord gave me nectar in a cup, the nectar of the true and holy name. Those who feast and take their fill of the Lord's holiness at the Gurū's bidding, attain peace and joy. Your minstrel spreads your glory by singing your word. Nānak, by adoring truth we attain all-highest (AG 150).

From that day he began to preach a message of the oneness of God, the potential for anyone, regardless of caste or sex, to

13

experience God's grace and receive spiritual liberation, mukti, even in this present existence without waiting for death, the state of jīvaṇ mukt, rejection of religious actions as a way of acquiring merit or salvation, and the replacement of the Hindu varnāśramadharma with the householder, gristhī, way of life. Spiritual development was to be concentrated upon the God-oriented and God-filled by keeping God in mind using a technique known as nām simraṇ. This was to be accompanied by kīrt karṇā, earning one's living by doing honest socially acceptable work, and vanḍ chaknā, caring for the needy by deed or gift. There is a sense in which Gurū Nānak, as he should now be called, was helping people to make a virtue of their necessity. The way of sannyās, the fourth stage of Hindu life, renunciation of family and worldly ties, was not an option for most villagers, even if they belonged to one of the twice-born castes which alone were allowed to practise it. The Guru was saying that the drudgery of village existence was not to be despised, avoided, and willed away, it was *the* path ordained by God through which one could become jīvaṇ mukt. Such teachings obviously won the support of many low-caste and outcaste Hindus but there is evidence that it also appealed to some twice-born Hindus, including brahmins, and Muslims.

Between about 1499 and 1521, Gurū Nānak undertook a series of journeys, known as udāsīs, which, according to the janam sākhīs, took him to such places as Tibet, Mecca, Sri Lanka, Burma, and many countries in between. The janam sākhī pericopes have a fairly set form of encounter, conversion (or occasionally rejection), and conclusion usually in the form of a hymn which he composed to meet the particular situation. For example, as the Gurū was walking along a road, a local robber, named Bhola, appeared and demanded him to hand over the only things he possessed, his clothes. Gurū Nānak asked him to find out from his family which he supported by his violent crimes, whether any of them would stand by him at the moment of death. Bhola returned in dismay, for they had told him that in his

14

encounter with death they could not help him, despite their indebtedness; what they owed him could be repaid only in this life. Realizing the limitation of material and human attachment Bhola returned to the Gurū grief and guilt stricken and asked how he might amend his ways and shed the karma of his evil deeds. Gurū Nānak replied, 'What use is any service, virtue or wisdom other than the divine Name? Worship the Name, only thus shall your bonds be broken.'

Sometimes the Gurū openly denounced hypocrisy as when he hid the begging bowl of a yogī who claimed to be able to use his spiritual power to tell the future, but was unable to discover where the bowl was! Or he would refuse to pray with a Muslim not because he was critical of Islam but on the grounds that the Muslim had not prayed as his intention, nīyat, was wrong; he was thinking about the price that his servant was getting selling horses in Kābul market, and not about Allāh. On these journeys he was often accompanied by a Muslim from his own village, Mardānā. Portraits often show another companion, Bhāī Bālā, a Hindu, but only one janam sākhī mentions him and some scholars doubt that such a person did take part in the udāsīs.

In 1521 or thereabouts, Gurū Nānak settled at a place called Kartārpur on the river Rāvi. There he established what is considered to have been the ideal Sikh community. Its focus was the Gurū and his message which the Panth would gather daily to hear. Some eighty years later, though perhaps still in the lifetime of one of its members, Bhāī Buḍḍhā, who is said to have lived to well over a hundred years, Bhāī Gurdās provided this description.

Bābā Nānak then proceeded to Kartārpur and put aside the garments of renunciation. He clad himself in ordinary clothes, ascended his gaddi and thus preached dharma to his people. He reversed the normal order by, before his death, appointing [his disciple] Aṅgad as Gurū [and bowing before him], for his sons did not obey him and became instead perifidious rebels and

15

deserters. He gave utterance to words of divine wisdom, bringing light and driving away darkness. He imparted understanding through discourses and discussions; the unstruck music of devotional ecstasy resounded endlessly. *Sodar* and *Āratī* were sung [in the evening] and in the early morning *Japjī* was recited. Those who followed him cast off the burden of the *Atharva Veda* [and put their trust in the gurbāṇī] (Bhāī Gurdās, Vār 1).

As the quotation also states, before he died Gurū Nānak decided to appoint a successor who was installed as Gurū three months before his death. The event is described by Bhāī Gurdās in some detail later in the same var.

Before he died he installed Lehṇā and set the Gurū's canopy over his head. Merging his light in Gurū Aṅgad's light the Sat Gurū changed his form. No one could comprehend this. He revealed a wonder of wonders, changing his body he made Gurū Aṅgad's body his own (Vār 1, pauri 45).

Lehṇā, one of the Gurū's followers, was chosen in preference to either of his two sons. He was renamed Aṅgad in a play on words of deep significance. 'Aṅg' in Punjabi means 'limb', Aṅgad indicated that the new Gurū was inspired with the same message as Gurū Nānak. Sikhs would not use the word 'reincarnation' but they are emphatic that the teaching was identical. In the scriptures this idea is endorsed by the way in which none of the other Gurūs who composed hymns uses his own name. Each uses the phrase, 'Nānak says'.

An apparently dramatic change took place in 1699 when, at the Baisākhī gathering, the tenth Gurū, Gobind Siṅgh, established the institution of the Khālsā and, with it introduced the concept of the saint-soldier. The arming of the Sikhs and his teaching that the use of armed force is permissible in the cause of righteousness, and his doctrine of the just war, the dharam yudh, have resulted in a contrast being made between him and Gurū Nānak which

16

neglects the first Gurū's opposition to the treatment of prisoners and non-combatants during Bābur's invasion, as well as Gurū Aṅgad's criticism of Emperor Humāyūn, and political interventions by Gurū Amar Dās against exacting a pilgrim tax from Hindus going to Hardwār. There is also the neglected fact that on such matters as equality, the rejection of caste, the status of women, social issues in general and theological principles, the two shared the same position. Sikhs would regard the 'one light' doctrine as being intact. To stress the contrast in such a phrase as 'from pacifist Sikh to militant Khālsā' is to highlight only one of Gurū Gobind Siṅgh's contributions, to neglect the fact that the movement towards militancy can be traced back as far as the time of the sixth Gurū, Hargobind, 1606 – 44, while the assertion that Gurū Nānak was a pacifist at best cannot be proven. As the leader of a small group of Sikhs numbering only hundreds it is unlikely that recourse to arms would have done more than guarantee the extinction of the Panth leaving no trace of it in the history of religion or India.

Gurū Gobind Siṅgh brought to its culmination the key doctrine of guruship. Gurū Nānak said that the words he spoke were not his own but were divinely inspired, 'As the word comes to me so I speak' (AG 722) and whenever he uses the word 'gurū', unless he is referring to other human preceptors, usually with scepticism, he is speaking of God. God is formless, niraṅkār, and incomprehensible, but chooses to become manifest as word, sabad, in the form of inspired utterances, the gurbāṇī. These were entrusted to the Sikh Gurūs but not exclusively. When he made the first compilation of the Sikh scriptures, the *Ādi Granth* in 1604, Gurū Arjan included the works of men like Kabīr, Nāmdev and Sheikh Farīd (the bhagat bāṇī), as well as some compositions by bards at his court. The bhagat bāṇī is of considerable theological significance. It may originally have been collected by Gurū Nānak, certainly it existed before the time of Gurū Arjan, and although one of its purposes may have been to attract Kabīr panthis and others to the new Sikh movement, its longer lasting importance is as a statement that God speaks through non-Sikhs and, within Sikhism, not only through the Gurūs. When in 1708 Gurū Gobind Siṅgh conferred guruship on the *Ādi Granth*, hence the name *Gurū Granth Sāhib* by which it is usually known, he was remaining faithful to the principles of the first Gurū.

However, the doctrine of guruship does not end with the Gurū Granth Sāhib. The tenth Gurū had also said that the Khālsā was his other self, that he existed within it but that it shared his authority as well. There are accounts of his bowing to the will of the Khālsā. This has resulted in the belief that God as Gurū is present in the community. The idea of the Gurū Panth may be neglected but should be remembered whenever Sikhs assemble in the presence of the *Gurū Granth Sāhib*. Again the beginnings of this doctrine can be traced back to Gurū Nānak himself.

History has, of course, had an influence in shaping the Sikh movement; perhaps it has been greater than on some other Indian panths because the Sikh Gurūs took material existence so seriously. There is no suggestion that the world is an illusion of no importance. God is creator, Kartā Purukh, as well as the Timeless One, Akāl Purukh, and is therefore manifest in creation and in history. The use of the term Sachā Pādshah, a Mughal imperial title, by Gurū Rām Dās and his successors, may say more about their involvement in politics than their aspirations to supplant the empire with one of their own, but the martyrdoms of the fifth and ninth Gurus as well as the imprisonment of the sixth were seen by the sovereign power as prompted by acts of treason rather than being the results of religious persecution. It is beyond dispute that these events and many others between 1606 and 1708 indicate an association of religion and politics which is seen in the miri-piri guruship of Gurū Hargobind and his successors, and above all in the principles of the Khālsā. Gurū Gobind Siṅgh's relationship with Emperor Aurangzeb varied; it was certainly not one of unmitigated hostility as has sometimes been suggested, but during the century following their deaths the Sikhs were usually found to be engaged in a struggle for survival which eventually swung their way and led to the establishment of a Sikh empire from 1799 until the British annexed the Punjab in 1849. The history of the Sikhs during this period and the political activity of the Gurūs must be studied and appreciated by anyone who would understand the events of the nineteen eighties.

Perhaps Sikhism is a religion which thrives on persecution. Be that as it may, a consequence of the period of religious liberty and tolerance, which coincided with the reign of Mahārājā Ranjīt Singh, led to the decline of the Khālsā ideal and a blurring of Sikh-Hindu distinctions. These caused little concern until the Punjab became the scene of Christian activity from 1834 followed by that of the Hindu reformist movement known as the Ārya Samāj. The Sikh response came in the form of the Nāmdhāri, Nirankāri, and Singh Sabbhā movements which led to a purification of Sikh rituals, educational reforms and the development of a new idealism related to a Sikh renaissance.

The Nirankāris owe their origins to Bābā Dayal, 1783 – 1855. In 1808 he broke with recent Sikh tradition by marrying without the services of a Hindu priest because none would perform the ceremony in the month Chaitra, a time believed to be inauspicious. The wedding took place in a gurdwārā, as it would have done, but instead of the priest's ministrations, the *Anand* and other passages from the *Gurū Granth Sāhib* were used. Some years later, on the day that a notable visiting Sikh preacher was to be honoured, one of his hosts suddenly died. Bābā Dayal decided that the meal, langar, should be held as arranged. The guest expressed horror at the idea of putting himself in a situation which would cause him to be polluted. The celebration was held, without the chief guest and many of his friends, though the next day Dēwān Singh acknowledged that his concern had been contrary to the tenets of Sikhism. Bābā Dayal's opposition to Hindu forms of Sikh weddings persisted up to his death in 1855, by which time the practice of circumambulating the *Gurū Granth Sāhib* four times during the reading of the hymn, *Lāvān*, had been introduced.

19

The place of the Ten Gurus in the Sikh religion

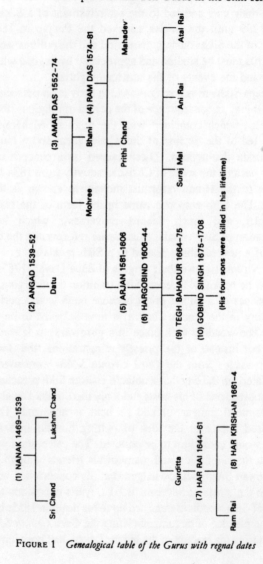

FIGURE 1 *Genealogical table of the Gurus with regnal dates*

The place of the Ten Gurus in the Sikh religion

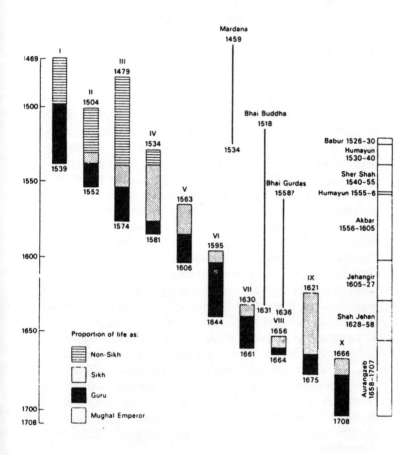

FIGURE 2 *The Sikh Gurus in their Mughal context*

While the Nirankāri thrust was against the permeation of Sikhism by Hindu beliefs and practices, the Nāmdhāris opposed moral laxity within the Sikh community. Bābā Balak Siṅgh, 1799 – 1861, founder of the movement, criticized the prevalence, within the Panth, of the use of drugs and alcohol, meat eating (which was not against Sikh tenets), sexual immorality, and personal extravagance at weddings, and the giving of dowries. He also supported intercaste marriages and the rights of widows to remarry.

The Siṅgh Sabhā movement was of greater overall importance as it managed to exert influence over the whole Panth, especially at the level of the more powerful members. The first association (which is what 'sabhā' means), was formed in 1873, in Amritsar. It could not therefore have been a response to the Hindu Ārya Samāj movement which did not come into existence until 1875 and only began to operate in the Punjab two years later — by Sikh invitation. The immediate cause was the conversion of four Sikh students in Amritsar in 1873, proof, if any were needed, of the threat to the Panth which began in 1852 when Daud Siṅgh from Cawnpore, the first recorded convert, began preaching the Christian Gospel. The aims of the movement were to purify the Panth of Hindu influences and educate it so that it could resist the arguments put forward by the missionaries. Pamphlets, books and educational institutions were the swift result. It was accompanied by demands for the legalizing of Sikh forms of marriage and the right of the community to own its gurdwārās, many of which had fallen into private, often non-Sikh, ownership. This eventually manifested itself in agitation leading to the Gurdwārās Act of 1925. This legislation vested control of the gurdwārās in the Punjab in the hands of a Sikh organization set up for the purpose, the Shromaṇī Gurdwārā Parbandhak Committee.

The independence of India was achieved only at the cost of the partition of the subcontinent which meant that the Punjab was divided between India and Pakistan with the capital city of

Mahārājā Ranjīt Siṅgh's state, Lahore, and the birthplace of Gurū Nānak, Talwaṇḍi or Nankana Sāhib, as it is now called, being included in Pakistan. Since then two issues have dominated Sikh history. The first is a concern for a state within the republic of India which can be regarded as Sikh. This has grown with the perception which many Sikhs have that their country is not one in which all religions are treated equally (Nehru's concept of a secular India), but one with a Hindu majority eager to dominate minority groups. Sikh reaction took the form of agitation for a Punjabi-speaking state, and this was eventually created in 1966, but without Chandīgarh, which had been built to replace the loss of Lahore, and some other Punjabi-speaking areas in nearby Haryānā. The dispute with the central government therefore continued with the major Sikh political party, the Akāli Dal, demanding the implementation of what is known as the Anaṇḍpur Sāhib Resolution of 1973. In the continuing agitation, more extreme Sikhs looked for a solution through secession from India and the creation of an independent Sikh state of K̲h̲ālistān. This issue remains unresolved at the time of writing, but it must be recognized that those who wish to leave the union, and those distressed and angered by the Operation Blue Star, when the Indian army entered the Darbār Sāhib (Golden Temple) in 1984, form the vast majority of Sikhs.

The second issue of importance in contemporary Sikh history is the development of and direction to be taken by the Sikh diaspora. This is a recent phenomenon which has not attracted much notice within the Punjab itself though it has resulted in its material enrichment in the form of money sent back to their families by Sikhs now living in North America or Britain. Soon after the annexation of the Punjab by the British in 1849 Sikhs began to move into other parts of India and later abroad. They moved with the army or civil administration. However, the first significant migration was to East Africa in the 1890s as workers employed by the British who were constructing railways and a general infrastructure to open up the hinterland of the ports. Then, in

1947 – 8 came the upheaval of the partition of the subcontinent of India which led to Sikhs from the region which became Pakistan settling in Delhi and other areas of India besides the Punjab. During the whole of the twentieth century Sikhs have been moving into English-speaking parts of the world, but the largest single migration occurred between 1956 and about 1973 when well over 100,000 went to Britain, first from the Punjab, for economic reasons, and then from Africa for motives which were usually political and economic, though those expelled from Uganda in 1972 could be regarded as refugees. There are now over 300,000 Sikhs in Britain. The total population of the Sikh diaspora may be as many as one million. How the Sikh religion will be affected by having eight per cent of its membership living outside India is hard to predict. The Sikh majority, those in the Punjab, have their own issues to concern them. Many elsewhere are striving to maintain a Punjabi-Sikh culture and identity, but there are also those who recognize that a reappraisal of Sikhism is necessary as a generation grows up which wishes to be Sikh but cannot be Punjabi, either because it has no wish to be or it is no longer practical. It is likely that any major changes in Sikh practice will happen in America or Britain and will not affect Sikh theology but will result in a form of Sikhism which may be nostalgically Punjabi or may consciously distance itself from its Punjabi origins.

In common with all the established expressions of religion and spirituality, Sikhism, in the west at least, finds itself in a world which seems to have little acknowledged need for it. Its response is one which the authors of this dictionary cannot predict and will not speculate upon but will watch with interest during those years which remain to them.

Major beliefs. The principal Sikh belief upon which all others are based is the oneness of God. Sikhism is essentially monotheistic. 'God is the eternal giver and there is no other' (AG 933). The main tenets of this concept are contained in the Mūl

Mantra, a terse statement enunciated by Gurū Nānak which is placed at the very beginning of the _Gurū Granth Sāhib_, included as a preamble to his most famous composition, the _Japjī_, and used in an abbreviated form to introduce divisions and subdivisions in the scripture. It is explained to initiates during the amrit ceremony. It begins with the figure One. A paraphrase reads as follows:

> This Being is One; the Truth; immanent in all things; creator of all things; sustainer of all things; immanent in creation. Without fear and with enmity. Not subject to time. Beyond birth and death. Self-manifesting. Known by the Gurū's grace.

God, the one eternal reality, is ineffable and beyond the categories of male and female though usually the male pronoun is used and never 'it', but, as the final phrase in the Mūl Mantra states, is self-revealing as Gurū, by grace. God is the supreme Gurū, known through the revealed teaching or word (sabad). The ten human Gurūs, who were born as the result of God's will (hukam), not their own karma, received and communicated this word. It is now contained in the sacred book of the Sikhs, the _Gurū Granth Sāhib_, which was installed as Gurū in 1708. The physical volume is the focus of worship in gurdwārās (Sikh places of worship), and must be present at most other religious ceremonies. It is treated with considerable respect because of the word which it contains.

God as Gurū is the self-revealing aspect of the divine whose purpose is to bring about the spiritual liberation of humanity. The natural state of human beings is one of ignorance. Whether their intentions are good or bad, their lives are consequently characterized by the pursuit of illusory goals. These are summed up in the five evils of lust, covetousness, wrath, pride, and attachment to worldly possessions and aspirations. They are victims of haumai (self-reliance, or egoism), and as such are doomed to the cycle of transmigration ('coming and going' is the

25

popular phrase of the Gurūs), until God's grace effects a liberating transformation and ends the cycle.

Such an unregenerate person is called 'manmukh'. Attitudes and actions are self-willed and self-centred. Even if they seem to be for the good of the extended family or society the motive is not one of obedience to God. To achieve liberation it is necessary to become gurmukh, God-centred, with one's thought and actions focused on and guided by, even determined by, the Gurū. This can only happen as the result of divine activity and initiative, God's grace. Sikhism is a religion of grace. God is sovereign, therefore there is a tension between human free will and divine omnipotence as there is in many other religions.

The state of liberation is possible here and now. It is possible to become jīvaṇ mukt, liberated while in the body. The karmic process must work itself out but no further accumulation of karma occurs. The purpose of life is transformed. Effort is no longer undertaken to achieve self-destruction or even liberation, but to serve God, to obey the divine hukam. Life becomes characterized by the practice of virtues which are innumerable though, because it is a popular number among Sikhs, five are sometimes listed — truth, contentment, compassion, patience, and dharma (the humble service of God and humanity).

The Sikh emphasis is very much upon practical religion and ethics. Gurū Nānak once said, 'Truth is the highest virtue of all, but higher still is truthful living' (AG 62).

The despised life-style of the peasant with its endless drudgery was commended as the true way of dharma. The burden of family was to be seen as the medium through which God was to be encountered and served. As Gurū Tegh Bahādur expressed it: 'Why go to the forest to seek God? God is to be found at home' (AG 684).

The four aśramas (stages of Hindu life), which ended in that of sannyāsīn (renunciate), when a man left the family to devote himself to the pursuit of the goal of liberation (mōkśa), were rejected. All stages became one, that of householder (grihastha, in Punjabi gristhi). The four goals (dharmas) of Hinduism, wealth, pleasure, duty, and liberation, became concurrent rather than consecutive. Of course the varnāśramadharma, as this is called, was open only to men, and they had to belong to the twice-born castes, brahmin, kśatriya, or vaiśya. The Sikh way of life was available to all, including women. The fundamentals of this life are summed up in three phrases, nām japo, kīrt karo, vaṇḍ cako, true worship, honest socially worthwhile work, and caring for the needy. 'The householder who gives all he can afford to charity is as pure as the water of the Ganges' (AG 952).

Begging is rejected, it confers no merit on the giver and no self-respect on the recipient. The needy should be helped to work. On the other hand sevā, voluntary service for the benefit of the Panth and humanity in general, is highly valued.

The *Ādi Granth* contains compositions by non-Sikhs, what is known as the bhagat bāṇī, men who were brahmins, outcastes, or Muslims as well as those like Kabīr who refused, like Gurū Nānak, to accept the name of any religion. The recognition of this material as scripture, the divinely revealed word, is a statement that truth is not confined to Sikhism. One may come across affirmations of exclusiveness made by Sikhs but one will also find interpretations of the Khālsā which say that it is not confined to initiated Sikhs but embraces all who know and serve the One God, 'the brotherhood of the Pure [Khālsā], is the brotherhood of the entire humanity' (Taran Singh, *Sikh Courier*, vol. 4, no 3., page 29, 1966).

Terminology. As Sikhism, along with other religions, exercises the minds of scholars and the attention of the media, the appropriate use of terms becomes a matter of importance. Attempts are made to help those who are uninitiated into the study of Sikhism by using such phrases as 'Sikh baptism', 'high priests', or 'the Sikh church'. During Operation Blue Star it was not unusual to see the Golden Temple described as 'the Sikh Vatican'! Ultimately Sikhism must be understood *sui generis*, the correct terms mastered, and the use of italics dropped, for if English is a world language it must be able to embrace within it amrit ceremony (if not amrit sanskār), jathedār, and gurdwārā. Reporters and authors of popular books and articles have to remember that even a word which they take for granted, such as baptism, may mean little to their audience in a non-religiously observant world. Serious writers on the subject of religion should be concerned for four other reasons. First, the terms used are usually Christian suggesting that this is the norm of religious studies. There should be no such judgement made; the reader might well be a Jew, a Buddhist, or a person of no faith at all. Terms should either be free of any religious bias, like 'initiation' for example, or, better still, specific to the religion being discussed. Secondly, it is frequently unhelpful. To refer to a Sikh granthī as a priest or initiation as baptism is only to set the student travelling in the wrong direction. Those who ask what sacrifice the priest offers or why Sikhs use the sign of the cross and whether the initiate is totally immersed are not the ones who are guilty of being awkward! Thirdly, it must be remembered that terms bring with them connotations. Not all Christians are happy with the idea of priesthood, they may actually regard Sikhism more favourably when they are told that the granthī is not a priest! Finally, however, if we are to understand a religion, any religion, it is necessary for us to free ourselves of our own preconceptions, prejudices, and stances, and as far as possible enter the thought-world of the tradition being studied, and this we are unlikely to do if we remain prisoners within our own language, for words are culturally conditioned.

A consequence of this consideration of the use of terminology is the conclusion that the name 'Golden Temple' is imprecise. We have therefore used the phrase 'Darbār Sāhib' which we hope will not be considered either a nuisance or an example of pedantry. We do not expect to succeed in persuading others to accept our position! Our reaction against 'Sikh Temple' might eventually be persuasive, and we are pleased to see that 'Sikh baptism' is

28

disappearing from usage in educational circles; perhaps the tautology, 'Sikh gurdwārā', will vanish too one day, but only when people cease to use 'Christian church' and 'Jewish synagogue'. Of course the usages of which we are complaining are those which we have employed ourselves though we hope not in this present publication. There is always scope for self-criticism and increasing sensitivity in such a young discipline as religious studies.

Spelling is another area where there is a heightening of consciousness and a state of flux. As non-Sikhs become more familiar with Punjabi they are increasingly inclined to search for the most accurate transliterations. So one comes across gurud-wārā, and vāhigurū, as well as Panjab. Sometimes Sikhs themselves do not agree on the most satisfactory rendering. The problems have recently been discussed by Eleanor Nesbitt, *Sikh Bulletin* number five, Chichester, 1988. In compiling this dictionary the authors have been guided by accepted Sikh usage but have borne in mind matters of correct pronunciation. The purpose has been to help the student, not to impose a form of spelling upon the tradition which we study. That is a matter for the Sikhs to sort out, if they wish to, however desirable the scholar may deem it to be.

Dating. Dates are given according to the Gregorian calendar. Where they are not suffixed by the abbreviation B.C.E. (before the common era), it should be assumed that they refer to the common era.

Abbreviations. The most commonly used is AG for *Ādi Granth*, followed by the number of the page from which the quotation is taken. As printed copies are uniform in their pagination no more detailed reference is necessary.

Bold lettering has been used in entries to refer to other relevant terms which the reader might find it useful to consult.

29

Diacritical marks have been used throughout the Introduction and in the first word of each entry but not elsewhere in the text.

Further Reading. A detailed introduction to the religion is provided by W. O. Cole and P. S. Sambhi, *The Sikhs: Their Religious Beliefs and Practices*, second edition, Routledge 1986, which has also been translated into Japanese and Polish (1987 and 1988 respectively). Many of the scriptural passages mentioned in the dictionary can most easily be found in W. H. McLeod, *Textual Sources for the Study of Sikhism*, Manchester University, 1984, which also includes the *Rahit Maryādā*. Detailed histories are Khushwant Singh, *A History of the Sikhs*, 2 volumes, Oxford U.P., India 1977, Harbans Singh, *The Heritage of the Sikhs*, Manohar, 1985, and Ganda Singh (ed.), *The Singh Sabha and other Socio-Religious Movements in the Punjab*, Patiala, 1984. Those wishing to gain an introduction to a janam sākhī should read W. H. McLeod *The B40 Janam Sākhī*, Gurū Nānak Dev University, Amritsar, 1980. The notes and commentary provide an excellent survey of many aspects of early Sikhism and Punjabi culture. The Darbār Sāhib at Amritsar naturally attracts much attention. The comprehensive study of it by Madanjīt Kaur, *The Golden Temple*, Gurū Nānak Dev University, Amritsar, 1983, examines its history, architecture, organization, and the rituals which are observed there.

Acknowledgements. As always, priority must be given to our wives, Avtar Kaur and Gwynneth, for their patience and support. Next, a word of gratitude must be expressed to Mark Baker who helped in choosing a word-processor and Paul Lyons and Norman Strange, Siân and Eluned, initiators in the art of using it. Amstrad are to be congratulated on producing such a user-friendly machine. Finally, thanks are due to the editorial staff of Curzon Press for their patience and success in turning the manuscript into a book. Any errors or omissions are the responsibility of the authors.

The maps and figures are reproduced from W. O. Cole and P. S. Sambhi, *The Sikhs: Their Religious Beliefs and Practices*, second edition, Routledge 1986 by kind permission of the publishers to whom grateful acknowledgement is made.

Ablution Sikhs reject the notion of ritual purity and **pollution**, the emphasis being on moral conduct, not rituals. Guru Nanak taught that 'True ablution consists in adoring God constantly' (AG 358). However, cleanliness for hygienic reasons is something of great importance. Bathing should be undertaken daily, before morning meditation: 'After bathing meditate upon your Lord with your mind and your body will become pure' (AG 611, Guru Arjan). An obvious consequence of this is that a Sikh will always have taken a bath before going to the **gurdwara**.

Should circumstances prevent bathing at least the face, hands and feet should be washed. This is known as panj ashnana (lit. five washings), this minimal act ensures that the dirtiest parts of the body, the hands and feet have been cleaned, and face-washing refreshes the whole body and removes drowsiness. However, even this should be done with the following teaching in mind: 'No amount of bathing can purify a mind defiled by falsehood. Ablutions are efficacious only if one lives truthfully' (AG 566).

Ādi Granth One of the names of the collection of Sikh scriptures. It was compiled by Guru Arjan who completed the work in 1604. Later, in 1690, Guru Gobind Singh added the hymns of the ninth Guru. Sometimes it is mistakenly suggested that the title was given to distinguish it from the **Dasam Granth**. However, not only does the name seem to have been in use before the latter book was compiled but also the word 'adi' does not mean first in an ordinal sense. Its meaning is cardinal signifying primal or original, c.f. the use of Adi Purukh, the Primal Being, as a name for God. Also the **Japji**, the most famous of Guru Nanak's compositions, begins with the statement that God is 'adi Sach(u)', true from the beginning (AG 1). Thus the Adi Granth is a way of expressing the belief that Sikhism did not begin with the ministry of Guru Nanak but has its origins in eternity. The eternal word **shabad** has been incorporated in the book (Granth). Since the time when guruship was conferred upon it in 1708, there has been a tendency to call the Adi Granth the **Guru Granth Sahib**

(which see for the main entry on the subject), but both names are used.

Adultery This is strongly condemned by the Gurus who encouraged chastity and marital fidelity, teaching that another man's wife should be regarded as one's own sister. Sikhs who have been initiated into the **Khalsa** must undergo reinitiation after expressing penitence if they have committed adultery.

Akālī One who is devoted to Akal, the Timeless Being, God. First used of the irregular armed Sikhs who resisted the Mughal forces in the late seventeenth century. They were also known as **nihangs**. The term Akali was revived in the period of agitation leading up to the Sikh Gurdwaras Act of 1925, when it was used of those who led the struggle for Sikh control of their gurdwaras. It now refers to a member of the **Shromani Akali Dal** political party which claims to represent Sikh interests at state and national level, though not all Sikhs support it. It is the majority party on the **Shromani Gurdwara Parbandhak Committee** which is responsible, under the terms of the Gurdwaras Act, for the organization and management of gurdwaras in the Indian states of the Punjab, Haryana and Himachal Pradesh.

Akālī Dal Literally 'the unified army of the **Akalis**', that is those who are devoted to the worship and service of Akal, the Timeless One. The name is a reminder of the struggle, initially for control of gurdwaras to be taken out of private, hereditary ownership, which took place at the beginning of the twentieth century, but which merged into the general agitation for Indian independence. The Akali Dal is now a political party with its base in the Punjab, which claims to represent Sikh interests. Its influence in the Punjab is considerable and it has often controlled the state legislature but in national politics it is regarded as only one of the many regional parties. It is the majority party on the **Shromani Gurdwara Parbandhak Committee** which manages gurdwaras in the states of Punjab, Haryana, and Himachal Pradesh.

33

The party, known also as the Shromani Akali Dal, is a reminder that Sikhs cannot accept the idea of the separation of politics from religion. Male members of the party often wear blue turbans, but this has never become so customary for it to be regarded as a reliable distinguishing mark. It was established on 14 December 1920.

Akāl Purukh The Being Beyond Time, or the Timeless One, is perhaps the principal term used theologically as a name for God, **Wahiguru** being that used in popular devotion. It affirms the reliability, constancy, and trustworthiness of God which is the foundation upon which faith is built. Guru Nanak frequently asserted that God was not subject to 'coming and going', that is the round of births and rebirths which characterizes the existence of human and other life forms. He declared, 'My God is ever new' (AG 660), that is changeless and unaffected by the ravages of time. 'Sky and earth will pass away, only the One will remain forever' (AG 64), is the way the fifth Guru expressed the same belief. This view also implies that God is neither born nor dies, something which is stated explicitly and emphatically in the **Mul Mantra**. The purpose is not merely to deny the Hindu concept of **avatar** but also to provide comfort and assurance, to encourage faith. So Guru Nanak teaches, 'You are the Timeless One, death does not hang over your head' (AG 1038), and it must, therefore, carry no threat for those who trust in Akal Purukh.

The name stresses that God is beyond temporal restrictions but Sikhism is equally emphatic that spatial limitations are also meaningless. God is transcendent and immanent, being omnipresent 'The one God is all-pervading and alone dwells in every soul' (AG 43).

God is personal in the sense of being compassionate or exercising power, but any allusions to physical form in passages in the **Guru Granth Sahib** are to be regarded as metaphorical. This applies to suggestions that God is male or female as well. It is customary to use the pronoun 'he' of God, yet the fifth Guru wrote, 'You are my father and mother, we are your children' (AG

34

268) and 'You are my father, you are my mother, you are my kinsman, you are my brother. In all places you are my protector, why then should I be anxious?' (AG 103).

Other verses by Guru Nanak, e.g. AG 1010 and 1021, reinforce this point, saying that God is not man, woman, or eunuch-like. 'God is also creator, Karta Purukh. Guru Nanak says, For countless æons there was undivided darkness, there was neither earth nor heavens, only the infinite Order hukam' (AG 1035).

The universe eventually came into existence as the direct result of God's will: 'When it pleased you, you created the world, establishing your creation without visible supports. You created Brahma, Vishnu and Shiva' (AG 1036).

God is also the true sustainer, destroyer, and re-creator: 'Having destroyed God builds, and having built destroys; having filled the sea God causes it to dry up and then fills it again. The One who is beyond anxiety has the power to do this' (AG 934/5).

As Akal Purkh and Karta Purkh, manifest in creation, God is both nirguna and saguna, without and with qualities, but in essence is **nirankar**, formless one. (See also **Sat Gur%u**.)

Akāl Takht A multi-storey building on the west side of the pool, sarovar, of the **Darbar Sahib** at Amritsar. The original construction was undertaken by the sixth Guru who established it as a seat of temporal authority in 1609, the spiritual focus being the Darbar Sahib. Often the starting point of political agitations and demonstrations. It contained many historical records and other documents which were destroyed when it was severely damaged in 1984 during Operation Blue Star. It is one of the five seats of authority in Sikhism, **takhts**. Its **jathedar** is regarded as enjoying a position of authority not possessed by the other four. He is final arbiter in matters relating to the **panth**.

Akhaṇḍ Kīrtani Jathā A group of Sikhs inspired by the teachings and example of Bhai Randir Singh, 1878 – 1961, a mystic and freedom fighter. They are punctilious in keeping the

Sikh form. Women not only keep all the **five Ks**, they also wear the keski, a small turban, under the headscarf (chunni). The spiritual emphasis is upon purity and meditation. Members are vegetarian and often take part in overnight performances of kirtan, devotional music, lasting twelve hours.

Akhaṇḍ Pāṭh An uninterrupted reading of the Guru Granth Sahib from beginning to end, undertaken by a series of readers to ensure that no break occurs. It is timed to take about forty-eight hours but should be conducted in such a way that there must be no haste and the words are read accurately, pronounced clearly, and can be heard and understood by the listeners.

In some major gurdwaras akhand paths are permanent features of worship, one beginning as another ends. Normally they take place at **gurpurbs**, ending before dawn on the day of the celebration. Families also arrange them on various occasions such as weddings, death anniversaries, moving into a new house or business premises. The reading is ended with a formal ceremony, **bhog**.

The origin of the akhand path is uncertain but it can be traced to the eighteenth century. In those turbulent times it would have been a means of uniting and strengthening spiritually, scattered and threatened groups. Its popularity doubtless increased with the availability of printed copies of the Guru Granth Sahib in the nineteenth century. Such readings have parallels in the Hindu tradition and these may have influenced Sikh practice.

Alcohol The Sikh code of Discipline, the **Rahit Maryada**, states that 'Sikhs should not partake of alcohol, tobacco, drugs, or other intoxicants'. The reason for this proscription is expressed by Guru Amar Das: 'By drinking wine one loses sanity and becomes mad; one loses the power of discrimination and incurs God's displeasure' (AG 554).

Ālūwālīā A Sikh member of the Kalal brewer or distiller caste (jati/zat). The name is derived from Jassa Singh Kalal,

1718 – 1783, a Sikh military leader, of that zat who came from the village of Alu, hence Aluwalia. Sikhs of the same caste-group have adopted it in preference to the Hindu name because ostensibly the link is with Sikh history and the **Dal Khalsa** rather than caste. The traditional occupation is one which members should not follow as it conflicts with the Sikh disapproval of alcohol. (The spelling 'Ahluwalia' is also found.)

Amar Dās, Gurū (born 5 May 1479, Guru 29 March 1552 to 1 September 1574). The uncle through marriage of Guru Angad's daughter whose influence led to his meeting the Guru and becoming a Sikh. He organized the community into twenty-two **manjis** or geographical divisions and also appointed women (see **peerha**) to undertake preaching work. To strengthen the cohesion of the Panth further, he introduced the custom of summoning Sikhs to assemble in his presence at the festivals of Baisakhi and Diwali. He also constructed a bathing place with eighty-four steps leading to it, known as a baoli, at Goindwal where his gaddi was situated, to provide Sikhs with an alternative pilgrimage place to Hardwar. The growing political importance of the movement may be judged from his successful intervention with the Emperor Akbar to secure the repeal of the tax on pilgrims going to Hardwar, and a meeting which he had with the Emperor. He was responsible for developing the institution of **langar**.

Amrit Literally nectar. This is made from water into which sugar crystals (patashas) have been stirred with a double-edged sword, a khanda, while certain scriptural passages are recited. It is used in naming and initiation ceremonies. Guru Nanak stressed the concept of amrit as **Nam** or **Shabad**, the name or word of God, rather than something material: 'God's word is true and sweet, the stream of nectar; whoever drinks it is emancipated' (AG 1275).

Guru Angad seems to have regarded God's name as the only authentic form of amrit: 'There is but one amrit, the Name, there is no other' (AG 1238).

Amrit bāṇī Literally, 'immortal utterance'. Sometimes the phrase is applied to the Sikh scriptures as in the verses, 'O God, your word is sweet nectar; hearing it I attain to the highest state of bliss' (AG 103 line 6), and, 'Listening to the Guru's word (amrit bani) removes impurity from the mind, and spontaneously lodges God's name in its place' (AG 665 line 3).

Amritdhārī One who has been initiated into the Khalsa in accordance with the rules and rites laid down in the **Rahit Maryada**, and who lives in obedience to the vows taken at the ceremony known as **amritsanskar**.

Amrit Pāhul A synonym for **amritsanskar**, which see.

Amritsanskār Also known as amrit pahul or khande di pahul, 'tempered with steel', it is the rite of initiation into the **Khalsa**. It should be undertaken only by those who are mature enough to appreciate fully the significance of the commitment being undertaken. There is no minimum age limit and sometimes the ritual has become a formality participated in by children.

A period of preparation should precede initiation during which the candidate begins to keep the Sikh form, **panj kakke**, and turban, in the case of males, as well as abstaining from those things which are forbidden to an **amritdhari**: cutting the hair, eating meat killed and prepared after Muslim custom, adultery, and using tobacco, the four **kurahts**, as well as committing other minor breaches known as **tankhas**.

The ceremony may be held in any place which is not a thoroughfare and where the Guru Granth Sahib is installed. The scripture is opened and amrit prepared by the **panj piare** while they recite the Japji, Jap, ten Swayyas, the Chaupai from the Dasam Granth, and six stanzas from the Anand Sahib, in the posture of soldiers ready for battle. Each candidate comes forward in turn and kneels in the same position. Amrit is taken in cupped hands and drunk; it is also sprinkled on the hair and eyes. When all have been initiated the remaining amrit is drunk by the candidates. They then recite the Mul Mantra and are told the vows which they must keep, the **kurahts**. Should any of these be broken the Sikh would be considered to be an apostate, patit; full reinitiation is essential after convincing the community of the sincerity of repentance. Breaches of the tankhas, sharing food from the same dish as uninitiated or apostate Sikhs, dying or plucking out white hairs (the natural form should not be tampered with), marrying a child for a dowry, or using alcohol or drugs, are dealt with by imposing an act of public penance usually of a menial nature. Ardas, the Sikh prayer concludes the ceremony, a **vak** is taken from the Guru Granth Sahib, and all present share **karah parshad** from the same dish. Initiates who have newly entered the Sikh religion are renamed in a naming ceremony.

Amritsar The city was founded by Guru Ram Das in 1577 though tradition associates it with Guru Nanak who is said to have meditated where the **Darbar Sahib** now stands. This, better known as the Golden Temple, was built by Guru Arjan whose successor constructed the **Akal Takht** nearby. Maharaja Ranjit Singh diverted the Grand Trunk Road to pass through the city which is now a major religious and commercial centre. Pilgrimage has no place in Sikhism strictly speaking but the city is revered and visited by many Sikhs because of its historic associations, especially at the festivals of **Baisakhi** and **Diwali**. (See also **Amritsar Massacre**.)

Amritsar Massacre At **Baisakhi** 1919 British troops under the command of Brigadier General Dyer fired upon a large gathering of people, mostly Sikhs, in an open space known as Jallianwala Bagh. There was only one exit blocked from the assembled Indians by the soldiers. An official report stated that 379 people were killed and a further 1200 wounded. The gathering contravened the Rowlatt Acts which gave the government emergency powers and declared such gatherings unlawful. It has always been argued that many of those in the Bagh, if not all, were unaware of the prohibition, having come to Amritsar from the countryside to enjoy the Baisakhi mela (fair). The massacre was certainly one of the most significant events in the independence struggle, and formed the prelude to Gandhi's non-cooperation movement of 1920 – 22.

Amritvēla An ancient Indian system of reckoning time divides the day into three-hour periods known as pahars. That coming immediately before sunrise is amritvela, the ambrosial hour, traditionally the most appropriate time for prayer and meditation. In the **Japji** Guru Nanak advised: 'Meditate on the glory of the True Name at amritvela' (AG 2).

The **Rahit Maryada** states that a 'Sikh is expected to rise early in the morning (at about 3 a.m.), and after taking a bath, meditate on the Name of God'. However, while obeying this injunction the words of Guru **Amar Das** must also be remembered: 'Those who engage in devotion do not wait to enquire when the hour will be auspicious; what kind of devotion is it which puts the beloved out of mind even for an instant?' (AG 34/5).

Anaṇḍ Bliss, the perfect state of equipoise which defies description and can only be experienced. It is said to be unique in that other conditions have opposites, for example good and bad, pain and pleasure, while anand has none. It is also the name of a composition by Guru Amar Das, sometimes known by the honorific title, Anand Sahib, found from page 917 to page 922 in the Guru Granth Sahib. Some of its verses are used in the naming and initiation ceremonies.

Anaṇḍ Kaṛāj Marriage is a highly important institution in the Sikh religion which affirms the householder, **gristhi**, way of life as the one through which spiritual liberation is found. The essence of the wedding ceremony is intentionally simple and brief though non-essential accompaniments which have no religious significance or sanction may take days or even weeks.

In 1909 the **Anand Marriage Act** was passed which made legal the Sikh form of marriage. The ceremony itself probably dates back to earlier times. **Nirankaris** would say it began with them, traditionalists would trace it to the Gurus noting that the wedding hymn, **Lavan,** is the composition of Guru Ram Das. The **Rahit Nama** of Bhai Daya Singh who lived in the time of the tenth Guru mentions Sikh wedding rites.

Marriage must be between two adults who have freely consented to it and should not involve the giving of a dowry. It may be solemnized on any day suitable to the two families but should take place in the morning. Any Sikh may perform the ceremony which need not be held in a gurdwara and in India usually is not. It must take place in the presence of the Guru Granth Sahib.

The couple and their fathers stand for the saying of the Sikh prayer, Ardas. They are then reminded of their duties towards one another as husband and wife. The **Lavan** is read stanza by stanza, it is then sung while the couple circumambulate the Guru Granth Sahib four times in a clockwise direction. When they return to their places after the fourth circling they are regarded as married.

Sikh marriages are monogamous; widow(er)s and divorcees are also married in the manner outlined above.

Anand Marriage Act, 1909 During the nineteenth century Sikhs began to react against the British legal requirement that they should be married according to Hindu rites, as Sikhs were classed as Hindus under the Indian civil code. It is claimed that Dayal Das, also known as Baba Dayal, 1783 – 1855, founder of the **Nirankari** movement was the person who revived the practice of marrying in the presence of the Guru Granth Sahib and reading the marriage hymn, Lavan. His own marriage, in 1808, was according to Sikh rites, but his son, Baba Darbara Singh, is accredited with having performed the first marriage ceremony as it is celebrated among Sikhs today, on 13 March 1855, at Rawalpindi, that is by circumambulating the Guru Granth Sahib during the reading of Lavan. The cause of the reform of Sikh ceremonies was taken up by the **Singh Sabha** movement.

The act states that all Sikh marriages conducted according to the marriage ceremony 'common among Sikhs called Anand' should be recognized as valid from the day of their solemnization as well as giving it legal status for the future.

Anandpur A town about six kilometres from the left bank of the river Sutlej in the Shivalik hills, built by Guru Tegh Bahadur. His son, Guru Gobind Singh, was there when he learned of his father's execution by the Mughal authorities and used it as a rallying point for his resistance to them. In 1699, at **Baisakhi**, the Guru ordered his followers to assemble there and dramatically founded the institution of the **Khalsa**. The Sikh martial tradition is remembered annually at the **Hola Mohalla** mela, an occasion for practising martial arts and visiting the many local gurdwaras associated with the ninth and tenth Gurus. The historic links of the town have resulted in its being called Anandpur Sahib by many Sikhs.

Anandpur Sahib Resolution In 1972, the **Akali Dal** met at Anandpur where it drew up a resolution which, it claimed, embodied Sikh aspirations. It covered a variety of issues, economic and religious, in the context of political demands. These ranged from land reforms to control of the waters of the rivers Sutlej, Beas, and Ravi, which were being used to irrigate the states of Haryana and Rajasthan, to the alleged detriment of the Punjab. Concern was also expressed at government policies restricting Sikh recruitment to the armed forces. Chandigarh should be included in the Punjab, areas bordering on the Punjab which were predominantly Punjabi-speaking should be transferred to it, and Amritsar should be declared a holy city. The particular issues served to bring attention to underlying concerns. These were: the slowing down of the green revolution, a sense of increased central government interference in the affairs of the State of Punjab, and a perceived favouring of Hindus to the disadvantage of minority religions in a nation committed to the ideal of equal respect for them all. The resolution formed the basis of Sikh demands during the subsequent period of agitation.

Anaņd Sāhib A famous hymn composed by Guru Amar Das. It celebrates his joy, or bliss, in finding the True Guru, hence the name 'Anand' and commends the experience and the life focused on God through **nam simran** to the reader or listener. **Anand**, or part of it, is used in a number of Sikh ceremonies. It occurs between pages 917 and 922 of the Adi Granth.

Anbhav prakāsh Enlightened experience. The perception of reality which is enjoyed by a person who has become **gurmukh** (God-centred).

Aṅgad, Gurū (born 15 April 1504, Guru 14 July 1539 to 29 March 1552) The second Sikh Guru enjoys the unique distinction of being installed as Guru before his predecessor had died. This action presumably demonstrates the recognition by Guru Nanak that the community should become permanent. Angad's original name was Lehna (sometimes Lehina is found), but was changed by the Guru to one which means 'my limb' and must have been used to indicate status. Guru Nanak had two sons: one, Lakshmi Das, was too proud, the other, Shri Chand, too ascetic to be the kind of leader he had in mind, but as a son often succeeds his father as Guru both might have expected to receive that honour, hence the care in indicating who the successor should be.

Angad became a Sikh during the last period of Guru Nanak's life when he settled in Kartarpur. Sixty-two of his hymns are contained in the Guru Granth Sahib but his main contribution to Sikhism was to give the **gurmukhi** script in which it is written its present form. His period as Guru was one of consolidation.

Ardās The petition of a servant to a superior, used as the name of the formal Sikh prayer which begins and/or ends almost every ritual. Ardas has three parts. The first is the historical calling to mind of the achievements of the Gurus, and other important Sikhs, as well as significant historical events; the second invokes blessings upon the Khalsa and all humanity; the third presents the special needs of the congregation to God and naturally changes

43

according to circumstances. A version of Ardas is found in the **Rahit Maryada** but slight variations are found in practice.

Arjan, Gurū (born 15 April 1563, Guru 1 September 1581 to 30 May 1606) The first Guru to have been born a Sikh and to have been a Guru's son, though not his eldest. Completed the building of the **Darbar Sahib** at Amritsar (the construction of the sacred pool, **sarovar**, had been undertaken by his father). He compiled the first authorititave version of the Sikh scripture, **Adi Granth**, in 1604, and installed it in the Darbar Sahib. Spurious versions of the hymns of Guru Nanak and his successors were circulating, and the **Panth** was spreading geographically, so there was a need for an authentic collection to be made available.

Relations with the imperial court during the last years of Akbar's reign were cordial and Sikh aspirations were high, but in 1605, Jehangir succeeded his father, Guru Arjan was arrested on suspicion of assisting the rival claimant to the throne, Khusrau, and was tortured. Although it is sometimes asserted that his death by drowning, in the river Ravi, was as a result of his treatment at the hands of the Mughals rather than by formal execution, he is honoured as the Sikh protomartyr.

Arorā A mercantile caste.

Artha One of the four **dharmas** of Hinduism. The acquisition of wealth (artha), is regarded as acceptable by Sikhs. However, it must not be seen as an end in itself. Tithing (**daswandh**) is encouraged, as well as generosity towards people in need. Greed and attachment are two of the five **vices** against which Sikhs are admonished. The Gurus frequently warned that wealth has only transitory value by such utterances as, 'Wealth does not accompany one after death' (AG 595).

Ārtī Hindu offering of light in worship. Guru Nanak responded to the elaborate arti ceremony which he witnessed at the temple of Jagganath in Puri, by composing the hymn **Sohila** (AG 13). It

44

offers a characteristic reinterpretation of the ceremony and also a cosmological vision: 'In the arti dish of the sky, the sun and moon are the lamps, the multitude of stars the pearls and jewels (which decorate it), the sandalwood trees are the incense sticks, the waving breeze, the **chauri** and the verdant words are flowers.' This is one of the verses which Sikhs should recite before they go to bed. They are also incorporated in the funeral liturgy.

Arya Samaj Literally, the Society of the Aryas. A Hindu reform movement which began in the last quarter of the nineteenth century. Besides countering the efforts of Christian missionaries it also attempted to bring Sikhs into the fold of Hinduism and was, therefore, with the missionaries, one of the stimuli which gave rise to the **Singh Sabha** movement.

Asceticism Emphasis upon moderation, the recognition of God as creator, and the Gurus' commendation of the householder, **gristhi**, way of life, result in condemnation of the efficacy of austere practices in pursuit of spiritual enlightenment or liberation. 'Attempts to subdue the desires through self-torture only wear out the body. The mind is not subdued by fasting and penances. Nothing else is equal to the Lord's Name' (AG 905).

Āsrama, ashrama A stage of human life. In the Hindu tradition there are four but Sikhism recognizes only one, that of the householder (**gristhi** in Punjabi). It is open to men as well as women, not only for the reason that its foundation is marriage, but also because Sikh theology regards men and women as equal.

Atman (ātmā) The soul. It is immortal and exists at one with God: 'God abides in the soul, and the soul abides in God' (Guru Nanak AG 1153). Whether this view of the relationship of the Soul and God is monotheistic or monistic is not absolutely clear. God, in Sikh teaching is **Karta Purukh**, the Creator, as well as **Akal Purukh**, the Being Beyond Time, so there is a strong element of transcendence as well as immanence.

Avatār (Punjabi, **avtāra**) The belief that God 'descends' (the literal meaning of avatar) to the earth to restore righteousness is unacceptable to Sikh teaching. God is continuously active in the world battling against evil through the divine word, **shabad**, and men and women who witness to God's Name, **Nam**. God is 'timeless and formless, beyond birth and death', as the **Mul Mantra** states. The avatars of Hinduism are seen to be human historical figures no more divine or enlightened than other people.

Bābā Grandfather is the literal meaning but it is used as a term of respect for old people generally. It is sometimes employed to refer to the Guru Granth Sahib.

Bābā Atal A gurdwara near the Darbar Sahib in Amritsar, built to the memory of Atal Rai, son of the sixth Guru.

Bābā Bakālā A small town about 40 kilometres from Amritsar, famous as the place where the eighth Guru, Har Krishan, said his successor was to be found. A merchant, Mukhan Singh, who had received a vision of the Guru during a storm at sea went to pay him homage after his safe deliverance and told the Sikhs who, out of twenty-two claimants, was the true Guru. The town is now a pilgrimage centre associated with the ninth Guru, Tegh Bahadur.

Bābur banī Between 1520 and 1526 the Mughal leader Babur made three incursions into India culminating in the establishment of his rule in Delhi in 1526. Four passages in the Guru Granth Sahib seem to allude to this invasion. They are found on pages 360, 417, 417 – 8, and 772 – 3, and are known collectively as 'utterances concerning Babur', that is the Babur bani. They are also contained in the **janam sakhis** in the context of narratives relating to the sacking of Saidpur. Their interest is twofold. First, they are rare examples of direct historical allusions in the hymns of Guru Nanak. Clearly the invasion moved him considerably, as might be expected if he witnessed it personally and was actually made captive. However, the second reason is even more important. The verses unequivocally state that Babur is an instrument of divine judgement. The Guru says, 'You spared Khurasan and spread fear in Hindustan. But to avoid blame, Creator, you sent the Mughal as death's messenger' (AG 360).

The belief that God is active in history may be implicit in much of Guru Nanak's teaching but nowhere is the idea as explicit as in the Babur bani.

Bairāgī An order of **yogis** (see **yoga**) which traces its origins to Bhatrhari, a ruler of Ujjain who renounced his throne to become a disciple of Gorakhnath. The Gurus taught that the truly detached ones (bairags) were those attached themselves to God while remaining within the family. 'They are blessed who are attuned to God through the Guru's word; they remain in the household, though in a state of equipoise. Nanak says they are truly detached (bairag) who are imbued with the Lord's Name' (Guru Ram Das AG 1246).

Baisākhī Second month of the Hindu calendar but the time of the spring harvest festival in the Punjab where it is also New Year. The festival known as Baisakhi usually falls on 13 April according to Gregorian Calendar dating. From the time of Guru Amar Das Sikhs assembled in the presence of the Guru and at this gathering in 1699 the tenth leader of the Sikhs founded the **Khalsa**. The occasion is now celebrated by a **mela** in Amritsar to which people come from most parts of the Punjab and beyond. It is traditional to begin harvesting only after the festival. This is also the time when the wrappings are removed from the **nishan sahibs** of gurdwaras and new ones put in their place. Gurdwara elections are often held at Baisakhi which may also be marked by initiation ceremonies, though **amrit pahul** may be conducted at any time.

Bālā, Bhāī A Jat Hindu companion of Guru Nanak on many of his journeys according to some traditions, and claimed to be the

47

author of one of the **Janam Sakhis**. Despite its considerable popularity and the fact that its date of the Guru's birthday, Kartik (November), is the one celebrated rather than a date in Vaisakh, favoured by most scholars, nevertheless it is to be doubted whether Guru Nanak actually had a companion of that name.

Balak Singh, Bābā (1797 – 1862)   Sikh reformer who encouraged simple living and the rejection of elaborate rituals, preferring instead the repetition of God's name, **nam simran** or as his followers called it, abhyasi, meditation on the name of God day and night. Marriages should be according to the Sikh anand ceremony, should not incur great expenditure, and no dowries should be given. Meat, intoxicants and begging were also to be avoided. His spirituality and message resulted in his acquiring a following which he provided for by designating a successor before he died, Baba Ram Singh. Because of their emphasis on nam members of the movement which has developed as the result of the work of these two men are known as **namdharis**.

Bālmīki   Punjabi form of Valmiki, the author of the *Ramayana*. He came from the sweeper, chuhra, caste. Early in the twentieth century many were converted to Sikhism hoping for social advancement which did not always result. Some have now attempted to establish an identity of their own which is neither Hindu nor Sikh but bears a resemblance to both. It is possible to visit a Balmiki Sabha, (the word is used in preference to gurdwara or mandir and means 'society'), where both the Guru Granth Sahib and the Ramayana will be installed side by side and many of the men will be **keshdhari**. There may be a picture of Bhai Jaita Ranghreta being embraced by the young Guru Gobind Singh on one of the walls. He it was who recovered the head of Guru Tegh Bahadur and brought it to the Guru at Anandpur. The Guru said, 'Ranghrete Gur ke bete,' 'Ranghretas are the Guru's own sons', but this act of service did not result in permanent social improvement.

Bāṇā The Khalsa uniform which consists of the **five Ks**, but with tight-fitting trousers, a sash round the waist, a long shirt worn outside the trousers, and a belt for the kirpan worn diagonally across the right shoulder.

Bandā Bahādur(1670 – 1716) Sikh leader in succession to Guru Gobind Singh, and martyr. Though the Tenth Guru was the last human spiritual teacher of the Panth, the need for political leadership continued. Banda Bahadur was captured and taken to Delhi where, with six hundred members of his army, he suffered execution rather than be converted to Islam. He became a Sikh upon meeting the last Guru. Born a Rajput, he was a Bairagi yogi until his conversion.

Bāṇī In popular usage an abbreviation of gurbani, a term used to refer to the composition of the Gurus and **bhagats** contained in the Guru Granth Sahib and so, sometimes to the book itself. Bani means speech or utterance but is confined to these spiritual writings.

Banno, Bhāī A Sikh who lived in the time of the fifth Guru famous for the copy of the **Adi Granth** which he made. He added the rest of the verse to the one line of a composition by the Bhagat **Surdas** (AG 1253), and also included a stanza by Mira Bhai at the end of Rag Maru. Guru Arjan crossed out both these additions and declared the copy 'bitter', that is spurious, comparison with the authentic 'sweet' version. It is known as the Khari Bir (the bitter version), or Mangat after the village of Bhai Banno. Another story suggests that the Guru was loath to allow his follower to borrow the newly-compiled Adi Granth but eventually said he could keep it in Mangat for one night only. Bhai Banno did so but spent a long time making the journey pausing to copy the manuscript on the way.

Bāolī A large brick well with steps leading to the water. The most famous it at Goindwal, the village of **Guru Amar Das**, who

49

was responsible for its construction. It has eighty-four descending steps one for each lakh (100,000) births which, according to Hindu and Sikh teaching, the soul may pass through on its journey to liberation. Guru Nanak spoke against places of pilgrimage and ritualism, but by this time second or third generation Sikhs, perhaps lacking the zeal of the first converts, needed to be weaned away from the custom of going to Hardwar. Tradition says that the Sikh who recites the **Japji** eighty-four times while descending the baoli and bathing in its waters will achieve spiritual liberation, mukti.

Bedī A khatri subcaste to which Guru Nanak belonged. It is variously regarded as being part of the kshatriya or vaishya varna in the Punjab. Distinctions are often blurred but it is certainly among the 'twice born'.

Benatī Literally 'a request'. Sometimes used as a name for an appeal for assistance made to Sikhs world-wide, as, for example, after the flooding in the Punjab in 1988.

Beṇī A Punjabi bhagat unknown apart from his three compositions in the Guru Granth Sahib.

Bhagat The Punjabi form of the Sanskrit Bhagavata, one devoted to the Lord (Bhagvan). Used of members of the bhagti (bhakti) tradition. In Sikhism refers to non-Sikh or Sikh non-Gurus whose compositions are contained in the Guru Granth Sahib. The former are **Jaidev, Sheikh Farid, Namdev, Trilochan, Parmand, Sadhna, Beni, Ramanand, Dhanna, Pipa, Sain, Kabir, Ravidas (Rai Das), Bhikhan, Surdas, Sunder**, and **Mardana**. Those who were musicians in the court of Guru Arjan are often distinguished from the former by the word bhatt, meaning bard. These were nineteen in number. They are Kal, Kalsahar, Tal, Jalap, Kirat, Sal, Bhal, Nal, Bhikha, Jalan, Das, Gayand, Sevak, Malhura, Bal, Harbans, Satta, and Balvand. Their swayyas (panegyrics), are to be found on pages 1389 to 1409.

Bhagat Bāṇī The general name given to material in the Guru Granth Sahib which was not composed by the Sikh Gurus. A full list of these bhagats and bhatts is given in the previous entry. Sikhs attach much significance to the Bhagat bani as a demonstration of the willingness of the Gurus to recognize that revelation was not confined only to them. Many would extend the principle to respecting all the world's scriptures and other expressions of spirituality.

Bhāī Brother, but used as a term of respect when referring to men of acknowledged learning or piety, either in the days of the Gurus or in later and even modern times. It is an epithet given by popular acclaim, not by formal decision. (Women are called bibi). Sometimes also used as a synonym for granthi or some other servant of the gurdwara.

Bhaktī One of the three major paths to salvation, or margas in Hinduism, the others being jnana marga, spiritual knowledge, and karma marga, ritual action. These two ways are denied any validity by Sikhs, as emphasizing élitism and the efficacy of such activities as pilgrimage, or the feeding of brahmins. The Guru taught the only basis for spiritual liberation to be faith in God who lovingly takes the initiative in seeking out human beings and transforming them. There is a popular Sikh saying 'If you take one step towards God, God takes a thousand towards you.' In this respect Sikhism comes nearer to bhakti marga than to any other form of Hinduism, and is often described as a bhakti sect by many Hindu and western writers. Sikhs dislike this description, which seems to question the distinctiveness of the revelation received by the Gurus. There are also tenets of the tradition which they reject, especially the belief in **avatar** which characterizes the most popular form of bhakti, Vaishnavism.

Bhātra A subcaste whose traditional occupation is said to have been begging, an activity which is unacceptable in Sikh culture, so Bhatra Sikhs have become pedlars and traders. It may be that large groups of them joined the Panth late in the nineteenth century, but this is not clear. They tend to observe the requirements of Sikhism more punctiliously than most other castes, their men being keshdari and the women dressing modestly. Numbers of them migrated to countries such as Britain even before the second world war and settled in ports, for example Manchester and Cardiff, establishing some of the first gurdwaras. They tend to remain separate, socially and religiously, from later migrants in an attempt to preserve their lifestyle.

Bhaṭṭ See **Bhagat**.

Bhīkhan A bhagat unknown but for two of his compositions which are included in the Guru Granth Sahib.

Bhog The ceremony at the conclusion of an **Akhand** or **Sidharan Path**. When **Mundavni** has been read prayer in the form of the **Ardas** must be offered, a **hukam** taken (this is a reading taken at random and respected as God's command to the congregation), and **karah parshad** distributed to the congregation. Bhog is also used of the conclusion of congregational worship. Its literal meaning is pleasure.

Bikram era The Punjabi form of Vikram, a king whose name has been given to a dating system widely used in India. (See **samvat** and **calendar**.)

Bole so nihal/jo bole so nihal A Sikh slogan, exhortation, expression of affirmation or agreement. It may be heard in a gurdwara when someone has given a stimulating address or at the presentation of a **saropa**, an honour bestowed upon a person who has served the community. Its precise meaning is uncertain. Common English renderings are 'Let everyone who is saved say' or 'Let everyone who is happy (in agreement) say'; to which the gathering should reply, 'Sat Sri Akal' (Truth is eternal), the universal Sikh greeting.

Braj Bhāshā (Bhāṣā) An Indo-Aryan language spoken in the region of Mathura in Uttar Pradesh, sometimes called Braj. Vrindaban, the birth place of Krishna lies within it. Much of the poetry of the sixteenth and seventeenth centuries on the subject of Krishna is in this language. Its influence is present in the compositions of Guru Amar Das and, even more, Guru Arjan.

Buḍḍhā, Bābā Tradition asserts that this disciple of the first Guru lived from 1506 to 1631, dying at Ramdaspur (Amritsar). He was given the name Baba Buddha, signifying a wise old man, by Guru Nanak, while still a boy. He took part in the installation ceremony of the next five successors. He was also the first granthi of the Adi Granth. He was sometimes called Bhai Buddha.

Buḍḍhā Dal The 'army of veterans' formed by Nawab Kapur Singh in 1733 to look after Sikh holy places, preach, and initiate converts into the Khalsa Panth.

Calendar The basis of the Sikh calendar is the one which has been in use in northern India for many centuries. It begins at **Sangrand**, the time when the sun moves from one sign of the zodiac to the next, in April, usually on the thirteenth of the month. It has twelve months. The Sikh celebration of **Baisakhi** is determined by this solar calendar, and coincides with New Year's Day, and in villages especially, sangrand is observed monthly by services in the gurdwaras. Other celebrations, that is those associated with events in the lives of the Gurus, Diwali, and Hola Mohalla, are regulated by the lunar calendar, in common with Hindu practice. This makes periodical use of an intercalary month, Adhikamasa. Confusion has been known to arise, especially over the date of Diwali, because of the inclusion of the extra month, and the refusal of the astrologers who calculate festival dates to predict them more than about fifteen to eighteen months ahead. (For example the calendar of celebrations for 2000 C.E. will not be made until April 1999 or thereabouts.) The lunar month is also used by **Nanaksar** Sikhs who observe the birth of

Guru Nanak monthly at puranmashi (full moon). Sikhs observe no weekly holy day. In India it is common for people to make daily visits to gurdwaras. Among those living elsewhere the practice has grown up of holding major events on the most convenient days, Friday sometimes in Muslim countries, or Sunday which is now almost universally a holiday. Some Sikh authors use the **Samvat** era for dating purposes but mostly the Gregorian calendar and Common Era have been adopted, sometimes with Samvat, abbreviated to S, or Bikrami, Bk, provided in brackets. For example, the birth of Guru Nanak according to the **Bala janam sakhi** which is the basis for celebrating it in October/November may be given as Kartik (or the alternative form, Kattak), puranmashi, S 1526, or 20 October, 1469 C.E.

The attitude to regarding certain days as lucky or unlucky, which is a common feature of popular religion in India, is stated in these words of Guru Nanak, 'While counting and determining auspicious days, we forget that God is above and beyond such considerations' (AG 904).

Caste The term is used somewhat loosely to cover two related but different aspects of Hindu society, varna and jati (Punjabi **zat**). Varna refers to the class into which one is born, brahmin, kshatriya, vaishya, shudra, or the fifth, outcaste, which is called by a variety of names. Jati is applied to the subgroup to which one belongs. It is usually occupational. In practice, for most people jati matters more than varna, the notable exceptions being the brahmins and the outcastes. The two important principles of the varna-jati system are purity (and therefore pollution), and hierarchy.

The Gurus condemned the system, emphasizing that the accident of birth should not determine a person's worth. Guru Nanak taught, 'Caste is preposterous and renown vain; only the Lord gives all beings protection' (AG 83). 'Recognize God's light within all and do not enquire of their caste. In the next world there is no caste' (AG 349).

In terms of caste it might be appropriate to say that the Gurus' concept of society was one in which the four varnas, four ashramas, and four dharmas of Hinduism were replaced by the single varna of humanity which included women as well as men and exceeded the boundaries of religion. The grihastha ashrama, **gristhi** in Punjabi, subsumed the other three, and the goal of moksha (**mukti** in Sikh terminology), was to be pursued simultaneously with artha, karma, and dharma.

The message of the Gurus has not been adopted totally in practice for a number of reasons but it is probably true to say that the system is weaker in the Punjab, especially among Sikhs, than in other parts of India, and is a way of preserving social distinctions and influence more than a structure based on concepts of purity and pollution. Outside India it sometimes manifests itself in the form of gurdwaras which are open to any worshippers but whose committees are dominated by one group. **Bhatras** and **Ramgarhias** occasionally incorporate the name in that of the gurdwara, e.g. Ramgarhia Sikh Temple, Birmingham. **Jat** gurdwaras may use 'Singh Sabha' in their titles. (See also **Āluwāliā, Arorā, Bālmīki, Khatrī,** and **Ravidāsi.**)

Chābiān dā morchā Agitation to wrest the keys of the Treasury (Toshkana) of the Darbar Sahib from the government during the agitation for control of gurdwaras in the early nineteen twenties.

On 16 November 1920, a representative body of Sikhs was elected consisting of 175 members to manage the gurdwaras. The government had approved its establishment but, in November 1921, the Deputy Commissioner of Amritsar took the keys from the gurdwara officials, thinking the committee to be illegal. After agitation by the Sikhs the government realized its mistake and restored the keys to the Darbar Sahib authorities.

Chamkaur A small town near Ropar in Punjab. Site of a major engagement between the forces of the tenth Guru and an army of Mughals and Hindu hill chieftains in 1704. Three of the original **panj piare**, Mokham Singh, Sahib Singh, and Himmat Singh, as well as two of the Guru's sons, Ajit Singh and Jughar Singh, died in the battle. The gurdwara at Chamkaur Sahib is a reminder of their martyrdom.

Chānanī A canopy placed above the Guru Granth Sahib as a mark of respect. In gurdwaras this will be part of the structure of the takht or palki (dais), made of wood or sometimes stone, when the scripture is installed outside; at a wedding for example, it will be made of cloth.

Charan Pāhul (charn pāhul) Initiation before the foundation of the **Khalsa** in 1699 seems to have been of the kind used by other religious groups owing allegiance to a guru. It involved the use of water which had been poured over the Guru's foot and collected in a bowl. The initiate might be anointed with it and given some to drink. Rattan Rai, an Assamese prince, was initiated in this way by the tenth Guru prior to his introduction of **khande di pahul**.

Chaupai A four-line stanza form used by some of the Gurus.

Chaur(i) A symbol of sovereignty. It may take the form of a bundle of peacock feathers tied together with string, yak hairs embedded in silver, or man-made fibres placed in a wooden holder. It is used by Sikhs to demonstrate respect for the Guru Granth Sahib. Whenever the scripture is in use either the reader, or another member of the congregation standing beside him/her, will wave it over the scripture. Also used when it is being carried through the streets to be installed for a wedding or Path. It should never be called a fly-whisk, its purpose is not functional but symbolic.

Chelā The disciple of a guru. It is used in the Guru Granth Sahib to refer to Sikhs but now 'Sikh' is preferred: it has the same meaning but is derived from the Punjabi verb 'sikhna', to learn, rather than the Sanskrit, and has the advantage of having specific application whereas chela may be used of the follower of any guru.

Chief Chalsa Diwan Sometimes also known as the Khalsa Diwan. A council set up in 1902, as a product of the **Singh Sabha** movement, pledged to cultivate loyalty to the Crown (i.e. Britain), and to safeguard Sikh rights in relation to other communities, for example, adequate representation in the services, especially the army. For many years it was the main voice of the Sikh community and the medium of its resurgence.

Chola Apparel which has been sanctified by its use by a Guru. Sometimes such relics as a cloak may be seen in one of the historic gurdwaras. One of Guru Nanak's cholas, a cloak, is displayed at Dehra Baba Nanak. Today the term is used of the coverings of the **nishan sahib** at a gurdwara.

Dal Army, used of the Sikh forces which opposed the Mughals and Afghans in the seventeenth century. Later applied to political movements or parties, e.g. **Akali Dal**.

Dal Khālsā On Baisakhi Day 1748 Nawab Kapoor Singh addressed the **sarbat Khalsa** suggesting the formation of a well-organized standing army to replace the Taruna Dal (army of the young) which gathered only in times of emergency. A **gurmatta** was passed setting up the Dal Khalsa under the leadership of Baba Jassa Singh Aluwalia. It was divided into eleven **misls**, units each with its own commander. They were:
Aluwalia, under Jassa Singh Aluwalia,
Fyzullapuria or Singhpuria, under Nawab Kapoor Singh,
Sukerchakia, under Naudh Singh of Sukerchakia village,
Nishanwalia, under Dasaundha Singh, standard bearer of the
   Dal Khalsa,
Bhangi, under Hari Singh, (his successor as leader had an
   addiciton to bhang, hashish, hence the name),
Kanhaya, under Jai Singh of Kahna village,

Nakkai, under Hari Singh of the region called Nakka near
   Lahore,
Dallewalia, under Gulab Singh of the village of that name,
Shaheed, under Deep Singh (it took that name after his
   martrydom),
Karora Singhia, under Karora Singh,
Ramgarhia, under Nand Singh.

Sikhs will often refer to a twelfth misl led by Ala Singh of Patiala,
named Phoolkia, but this was not part of the Dal Khalsa.

Recruits could join the misl of their choice. These were not
equal in size, though the name is derived from an Arabic word
meaning equal. The total number of troops in the Dal Khalsa is
estimated at 70,000.

In 1978 Giana Zail Singh backed the foundation of a new
political party in the Punjab to oppose the Akali Dal. It was given
the name Dal Khalsa.

Damdama Sāhib   A place sanctified by the stay of a Guru,
therefore many gurdwaras are so named. The most famous is one
of the five takhts, situated at Talwandi Sabo, near Bhatinda. Guru
Gobind Singh lived there for about a year during which time, in
1704, he supervised the final recension of the Guru Granth Sahib.

Darbār Sāhib   Known more commonly by non-Sikhs as the
Golden Temple. Harmandir Sahib (Temple of God) is also used
frequently. Darbar Sahib means Divine Court. This is the most
famous of all Sikh shrines and the one to which they are most
attached both spiritually and emotionally. Pictures of it are to be
found in many homes in India and elsewhere. Since its foundation
it has been regarded as a major source of inspiration and, for
many, has become a place of pilgrimage. It stands in the middle
of an artificial lake some one hundred and fifty metres square. A
causeway about sixty metres in length links it to the marble
parkarma or walkway which runs along the edge of the lake. The
building is made of marble and is capped by a dome covered in

58

gold leaf. It is entered by four doorways symbolizing its openness to all people regardless of which of the four varnas they belong.

The present structure's doors, dome, and ornamentation belong to the time of Maharaja Ranjit Singh who embellished the building constructed by Jassa Singh Aluwalia in 1764. However, it was the third Guru Amar Das who conceived the idea of such a focus for Sikh worship, and his son, Ram Das, who commenced work on it in 1577. He did not live to see its completion which took place in 1601. In 1604 the newly-compiled Adi Granth was housed there with Bhai Buddha as granthi. Its importance to Sikhs has led to its being the site of conflicts on a number of occasions, the most recent being in 1988. In 1740 the Mughal governor of Amritsar desecrated it by using it as a dance hall; in 1762 it was destroyed and the pool (sarovar) filled in.

Worship in the Harmandir Sahib is almost continuous, beginning at about 4.00 a.m., and not ending until nearly midnight. Although the name 'temple' will persist it is not really appropriate in this context any more than it is when applied to other gurdwaras. It is supervised by a granthi whose functions in no respects correspond to those of a priest in either the Hindu or Christian traditions.

Darshaṇ (darśaṇ) In Hinduism the auspicious viewing of a statue of a deity, or the vision of one, or of a person, for example a guru. In Sikhism it may be applied to seeing the Guru Granth Sahib or hearing the words contained in it. In the Guru Granth Sahib itself it tends to be used of beholding or experiencing God. Interestingly, the word of Arabic origin, 'nadari', is also used, with the same meaning. Darshan is also employed to refer to the six orthodox Hindu philosophical systems.

Dasam Granth The collection of writings attributed to Guru Gobind Singh and collected by **Bhai Mani Singh**. The book was not completed until 1734 and probably also contains compositions by poets who were attached to the Guru's court. It is written in the **gurmukhi** script though the language of particular compositions may be Persian, Sanskrit or Hindi.

The book lacks thematic unity, not all its contents are religious, but it is regarded as canonical. The Jap and the thirty-three swayyas of the tenth Guru which are contained in it are used in initiation ceremonies. It contains over two thousand poems and in its printed form is 1428 pages long.

Daswandh The giving of one-tenth of one's income to the service of the Panth. The practice was begun by Guru Amar Das and was an obligation placed upon all true Sikhs. Its collection is no longer organized as it was in the times of the Gurus and is now in the form of a freewill donation. Whenever Sikhs visit the Gurdwara they will place an offering on the ground in front of the Guru Granth Sahib and may also guarantee to pay an annual amount to maintain the gurdwara and the services it provides as well as the charities which it supports.

Death Belief in rebirth means that death has not the finality which sometimes attaches to ideas that the present life is the only one. It is like passing from one room to another as part of a journey. Of course, in everyday practice bereavement is distressing and funerals are often accompanied by considerable public weeping, though there is an injuncture against loud lamentation in the **Rahit Maryada**. It should be remembered that, 'The dawn of a new day is the herald of a sunset. Earth is not your permanent home' (AG 793).

In the **Sohila**, used in evening devotions, the aim of life is set out as follows: 'Know the real purpose of being here, gather up treasure under the guidance of the Sat Guru. Make your mind God's home. If God abides with you undisturbed you will not be reborn' (AG 13).

Death ceremonies At the deathbed the **Sukhmani** should be read. Cremation is the preferred method of disposal and should be carried out on the day of death unless it is too late for the ceremony to be performed before sundown. The body should be fully dressed and should bear the Sikh emblems, the five Ks, and the turban if the deceased is a man. The preparation of the body is undertaken by family members in the Punjab and abroad, as far as is possible. Where local custom prevents cremation the body may be buried. Guru Nanak refused to express an opinion on the form of disposal, indicating that it is the spiritual state of a person that determines the nature of the existence beyond death, not how the last rites have been carried out. However, it should be done as quickly as decency allows. Delays caused by such things as post-mortem requirements are distressing, the whole notion of post mortem is offensive. During the funeral **Sohila** should be read. Ashes should be scattered in the nearest river but there is some tendency to take them to Kiratpur and put them in the river Sutlej. It is customary to hold a sidharan path, a non-continuous reading of the Guru Granth sahib, and for friends and relatives to gather for the **bhog** ceremony which ends at nine days after the funeral. In newspaper announcements this will often be referred to as Antimardas, meaning 'final Ardas'; friends and relatives will make a special effort to be present on this occasion. The family of the bereaved often make gifts to the gurdwara or charities as thank offerings for the life of the departed.

The practice of taking the body into the gurdwara at the funeral is now occurring in some British communities as is the commencement of an akhand path or sidharan path before the funeral has taken place.

Deep Singh   One of the great heroes and martyrs. He had been a member of the **Dal Khalsa** and leader of one of the misls but in his old age he devoted himself to making copies of the Guru Granth Sahib. In 1762 Ahmed Shah Abdali destroyed the **Darbar Sahib**. Baba Deep Singh announced his intention of liberating the site and rebuilding the temple. With his volunteer army he fought a battle at Guru ka bagh in Amritsar, and though mortally wounded in the neck, managed to reach the precincts of the Darbar Sahib. He died in 1757.

Deg Teg Persian words meaning kettle and sword. In Sikhism it signifies the dual responsibility of the Panth to provide food and protection for the needy and oppressed. Guru Gobind Singh spoke of charity, deg, and the kirpan, power, going hand in hand. (Dasam Granth p. 322). In the Sikh prayer, Ardas, is the phrase, 'Deg, tegh, fateh', 'victory to charity and arms'. This is also expressed symbolically when, at that point in the prayer, the **karah parshad** is touched with a kirpan.

Ḍerā A camp. The term is often used of the temporary or semipermanent settlement used by **nihangs** but also of the residence of a **sant**. This may include a gurdwara, the sant's own home, a communal cooking area, and accommodation for his followers, either as visitors or as permanent companions and aides. It corresponds to the ashram to the Hindu tradition.

Dhādī A folk-singer specializing in ballads of the royal and wealthy. One of the instruments used is the hand drum, dhad, from which they get their name. In the gurbani used of one who sings the praises of God. Guru Amar Das applied it to himself: 'I, a bard of the Lord called outside his door. The Lord listened from within to my plaintive cries and summoned me into his presence. "What brings you here, my bard?" he asked. "Merciful Lord, grant me the gift of (uttering) your name", I said. The benevolent one granted my prayer and blessed me with a robe of honour' (AG 91).

When Guru Nanak described himself as a minstrel he used the same term (AG 150).

Dhannā A vaishnavite jat from Rajasthan who is said to have been a disciple of **Ramanand**. Three of his compositions are included in the Adi Granth.

Dharam Yudh War in the defence of righteousness is regarded as proper by Sikhs. The tenth Guru actually said, 'I have no other ambition than to wage the war of righteousness (dharam yudh).'

In this, Sikhs assert, he was only pursuing the policy of Guru Nanak, who spoke out against tyranny, by other means. The interpretation of these words is that it was only such a struggle that could be justified, not one undertaken for self-aggrandisement. Guru Gobind Singh laid down five conditions of such a war. They were,

1. It should be as a last resort: when all other means have failed it is permissible to draw the sword (Zafarnama).

2. War should be waged without enmity or desire for revenge.

3. Territory should not be annexed, and property captured in the course of the war should be restored. Looting or the taking of booty are strongly forbidden.

4. The army must be made up of soldiers committed to the just cause. Mercenaries should not be employed and discipline must match the righteousness of the war. Sikhs are called to be saint-soldiers. The **Rahit Namas** command them 'not to drink or smoke, not to molest the women folk of your adversaries'.

5. These conditions being met war might be engaged in with the minimum of force used to achieve the objective, but regardless of the odds or the outcome.

It has sometimes been asserted that Guru Nanak was a pacifist. There is no evidence to support this view. He stated the principle that oppression should be resisted by asking the Emperor Babur to release the prisoners he had taken in capturing Saidpur and reminding him of a duty to rule with justice. Guru Amar Das required members of the Kshatriya caste not to neglect its dharma of providing people with a protective fence of justice (AG 1411). Sikhs argue that Guru Gobind Singh's use of military force was simply a change of method, not of principle.

Dharma A term with many meanings when used in Hinduism. The most common usage by Sikhs are: (1) religion or teaching, as in Sikh dharma; (2) conduct or lifestyle. In Hinduism this varies from one caste group to another. It also refers to the four goals of life, the pursuit of wealth, artha, earthly love, kama, dharma itself, conduct, and finally liberation, moksha, an occupation to which the other three should finally give way. Sikh teaching is that the four dharmas should be followed simultaneously, are the same for everyone, and apply to women as well as men. The essence of Sikh teaching on the matter is that all human beings should dedicate their lives to the one God and the service of their fellow human beings regardless of creed, class, or sex.

Guru Nanak taught, 'Those who wish to find a seat in God's Court should dedicate themselves to serving people in this world' (AG 26).

Dharmsāla The name given by Sikhs to the rooms or buildings which they used as for worship and other gatherings in the times of the earlier Gurus. Eventually replaced by the term gurdwara, though **Namdharis** still retain it. Literally a place where dharma is practised. In India commonly used of a hostel for pilgrims.

Dīwālī A major Hindu festival celebrated from the thirteenth day of the dark half of Asvina to the second of the light half of Kartikka, (October/November of the Gregorian calendar). The name derives from the Sanskrit 'dipavali', a row of lights. Sikhs remember that from the time of Guru Amar Das the Gurus summoned them to assemble before them on Diwali (as well as Baisakhi), that in 1577 the foundation stone of the Darbar Sahib was laid at the Diwali gathering, and that Guru Hargobind was released from imprisonment at Gwalior fort at the time of this festival in 1619. The custom of illuminating the Darbar Sahib at Diwali dates from this time. Clay oil lamps or candles are often lit on the steps of gurdwaras and firework displays held as part of local celebrations, as at the Golden Temple.

Dīwān (Dewān) In early Arab usage it was a land register or department of administration, but later came to be used of an assembly held for the purpose of administering justice and giving audiences to plaintiffs. In Sikhism the congregational gathering for worship is called diwan. The place in a large gurdwara complex where diwan is held may also be referred to as the diwan hall.

Doāb The land which lies between two (do) rivers (ab). Used especially of the area between the Sutlej and Beas.

Dōli The formal departure of the newly-married couple from the bride's home after the wedding. The bride was carried in a palanquin or sedan chair, a doli, but now she usually travels by car. Wedding invitations may mention the time of the doli, indicating when the couple will leave the reception. Doli can also refer to the songs which are sung at this time by the bride's relatives and to the highly ritualized departure itself.

Dowry The **Rahit Maryada** declared the demanding and giving of dowries to be against Sikh teaching many years ago and the practice was condemned earlier by **nirankaris** as contrary to the teachings of the Gurus. However, in common with many Indians, the dowry system is still found among Sikhs, even though it is now illegal, though there are also Sikhs who refuse to succumb to social pressures in this matter.

Dress There are few specific rules regarding dress. The main one is that the five Ks (**panj kakke**) should be worn and that men should wear the turban. Another is that modesty should be observed. This, with a line in the Guru Granth Sahib warning against clothes which 'cause pain to the body or breed evil thoughts' (AG 16), has resulted in the criticism of women for wearing short skirts or ostentatious saris. Tradition also encourages women to cover their heads with a dupatta or chuni, a length of cloth rather like a head scarf, especially in the presence of men who are not family members. In the gurdwara the head should always be covered.

On his journeys Guru Nanak dressed in a way that defied those who wished to place him within either the Hindu or Muslim traditions of holy men. When he settled in Kartarpur he put on the clothes of a householder.

Drugs One of the most serious prohibitions is that against taking drugs other than those which can be classed as necessary for medicinal purposes. It is recorded that after the sacking of Saidpur (Eminabad) Guru Nanak was taken into the presence of Babur the founder of the Mughal Empire who offered him a cup containing opium. He refused it and composed the following verse: 'Fear of the Lord is my opium, and my mind the container. I have become an intoxicated hermit. My hands are the cup. I hunger for your vision, O God, begging daily at your door' (AG 721).

Emblems See **Ik oaṅkār** and **Khaṇḍā**.

Enlightenment See **Mukti**.

Ethics Sikh ethics are wide ranging in scope, covering such aspects of life as **dress, smoking**, and **drugs**, as well as the rejection of **caste**, the equality of **woman** with man and the legitimate use of outward force as a last resort (**dharam yudh**). This is because Sikhism is seen to be a total life-style. Certain principles should govern all behaviour. They are, equal respect for everyone, truthful living resulting in earning it by honest means, moderation, helping the needy, serving the community, **seva**, and being a family person. The **gristhi** way of life, not that of the **sannyasin**, is that to which the Sikh is called.

Guru Nanak commended 'nam, dan, isnan', meditation (**nam simran**), almsgiving, and cleanliness (probably both physical and moral), as the way of life for the Sikh. Today these are expressed as 'nam japna, kirt karna, vand chakna', meditation, work, and almsgiving, but the emphasis upon a properly balanced life remains unchanged.

Farīd, Sheikh (1173 – 1263) A Sufi who lived in the Punjab and has become one of its most famous Muslim pirs. Guru Nanak met a man of this name at Pak Pattan and it is likely that it was adopted by all leaders of the community which the first sheikh founded. One hundred and thirty-four hymns attributed to Sheikh Farid are in the Adi Granth. They occur in two blocks, under Rag Asa and Rag Suhi.

Food and **Drink** Apart from a total prohibition on the use of alcohol, certainly by **amritdhari** Sikhs, there are no restrictions on what may be drunk. Meat slaughtered according to Muslim practice is also forbidden but Sikhs are not required to be vegetarian, though many are. This, and the tendency not to eat beef, is to some extent a consequence of living in a predominantly Hindu culture but often the reason has also to do with ideas about healthy eating. The concept of pollution should have no place in arriving at a decision about vegetarianism. In gurdwaras only vegetarian food is served. Guru Nanak himself once said, 'Only fools wrangle about eating or not eating meat' (AG 1289). Union with God, which in his view, was unrelated to such matters, was what concerned him.

Force, use of One of the principles of the **Khalsa** is that outward force may be used if all other methods of resisting tyranny have failed. However, this must always be as a last resort and traditional teaching is that the Sikh should never be the first to draw the sword, but having done so it should not be sheathed until it has shed blood. The meaning of this is that weapons should never be used to threaten or terrorize. When force is used it must be according to a strict code of discipline. (See also **dharam yudh**.)

Gaddī The seat or throne of a guru. It is used of a place and also of the office, so, for example, it can be said that Guru Angad succeeded to the gaddi of Guru Nanak.

Gambling Gambling is disapproved of because it is a form of exploitation and it also conveys the impression that the world is ruled by chance whereas it is subject to the divine will (see **hukam**).

Ghadr movement An association of Indians, mainly Sikh and Hindu living on the Pacific coast of America, which attempted to provoke a rebellion (ghadr) against the British in India during the first world war.

Giānī Literally a person of spiritual knowledge who has achieved unity with God. The term has been used traditionally as a prefix to someone's name. Now, however, it is also a minor academic qualification in Punjabi language and literature which need not include a study of the Sikh scriptures. The word has lost much of its prestige and respect in recent years.

Gobind Siṅgh, Gurū (born 22 December 1666, Guru 11 November 1675 – 7 to October 1708) Gobind Rai, as he was originally called, succeeded his father, who had been executed in Delhi, to the gaddi in 1675. The period of his leadership was one of the most eventful in the history of the Sikhs and by the time of his death at the hands of an assassin in Nanded, in the Deccan, the religion had assumed many of the aspects which characterize it today. He is remembered for three achievements in particular. First, in 1699, he created the institution of the Khalsa, recognizable by its appearance. The wearing of the turban and the five Ks have now become the hallmark of the Sikh. Members also adopted the name Kaur or Singh, hence the Guru is known as Gobind Singh rather than Rai. Secondly, he sanctified the use of military force, though only in the defence of justice, the dharam yudh. Finally, before his death he declared that the **Adi Granth** should be the only visible Guru of the Sikhs and installed it as his successor.

Guru Gobind Singh was a prolific poet as well as a soldier. However, he did not include his compositions in the Adi Granth. They are to be found, together with the works of some of the court bards, in the **Dasam Granth** compiled after his death by Bhai Mani Singh.

God The Sikh concept of God is at the same time simple and highly complex. In terms of simplicity God is one. 'There is no other' is a recurrent phrase in the hymns of Guru Nanak especially. However, this is not to be regarded as an affirmation of monism for God is also transcendent, creative, the universe is a manifestation of divine power, and gracious, being self-revealing in order to save humanity. Many names are used of God, including the Hindu, Ram and Hari, and the Muslim Allah and Khuda; they are, however, in a sense only names for the One. 'The One, who has created the forms of Vishnu, Brahma and Shiva, is the doer of deeds' (AG 908).

God is **Akal Purukh**, the Being Beyond Time or the Timeless One, the Eternal who exists in a realm distinct from all other beings who are subject to time, death and transmigration. God is also **Karta Purukh**, the Creator, who has brought them into existence. Though ultimately ineffable God is known to humanity through the Divine Word (**Shabad**), and is therefore called the **Sat Guru** or sometimes just Guru, or Sat Nam, for it is through grace and meditating on the Name that liberation is obtained.

Guru Gobind Singh taught that it might be necessary to take up arms in the defence of justice (see **dharam yudh**), and often used the epithet Sarab Loh, All Steel, of God. A popular name for God is Wahiguru, Wonderful Lord, which was originally a word used in praise of God as Guru.

Golden Temple See **Darbār Sāhib**.

Gorakhnāth Reputed founder of the **Nath** sect of yogis. He is mentioned in a number of janam sakhis, usually with respect, and in one, known as B40, inspires Guru Nanak to choose his successor. In another tradition, that of *Mahima Prakash*, he is the first person to recognize the Guru's greatness. However, the two could never have met. Gorakhnath's period is uncertain, but the latest date given for his death is the end of the twelfth century. In the Guru Granth Sahib the teachings associated with his followers receive severe criticism so one is left to conjecture whether the different treatment in the janam sakhis, which were written some time after the lifetime of the Guru, might not indicate a desire in the growing Sikh Panth to accommodate people who were attracted to his teachings which were a form of **hatha yoga**.

69

Got An exogamous group within an endogamous group called a **jati** or **zat**.

Grace 'The body takes birth because of karma, but liberation is attained through God's grace' (AG 2). These words aptly summarize the Sikh teaching about good works and grace. The Gurus accepted the Hindu concepts of karma and samsara, recognizing that the sound ordering of society required a sense of responsibility for one's actions. They acknowledged that such living, in which they stressed truthfulness and honesty rather than ritualistic purity, brought a reward, that of a higher and eventually human birth. In this respect, 'One reaps what one sows' (AG 662). However, such an attitude, if carried into the spiritual realm, could produce a mechanistic doctrine of liberation which rendered the need for God redundant, save perhaps as an object of devotion. This ran contrary to Guru Nanak's experience and understanding of God who had taken him, a person 'neither chaste nor true, not even a scholar, born into the world foolish and ignorant' (AG 12), and made him one through whom the divine message was revealed. Throughout his hymns and those of his successors the emphasis is strongly upon grace, the unmerited transforming power of God. A variety of words are used, karam from the Arabic, mihar from Persian, as well as kirpa and prasad from his own language and originally Sanskrit. Nadar, which he uses one hundred and fifteen times, may provide the clue to Guru Nanak's concept of grace. This word of Arabic origin refers to the favourable glance bestowed by a superior on an inferior and can be used of the divine-human relationship. Sikhism speaks of God as Guru. One of the major actions of a guru is to initiate the disciple's enlightenment by a glance which penetrates to the centre of his or her being. Darsan, from the Sanskrit darshan, is the word popularly used. It occurs forty-six times in Guru Nanak's hymns.

Grace is the beginning of the liberation process, through meditation on God's name, nam simran, the company of other enlightened people, the sat sangat, and the performance of good deeds, sewa, as a response to grace, the personality becomes transformed and one becomes jivan mukt, liberated while in the human body. 'Within us are ignorance, suffering and doubt, but they are cast out by the Guru's wisdom. The one to whom you show your grace and bring to yourself, that one meditates on the Name. You are ineffable, immanent in all. The one you bring to the truth is the one who attains it' (AG 1291).

Granth Book or volume. Sometimes used as an abbreviation for Guru Granth Sahib, but not recommended.

Granthī One who reads the Guru Granth Sahib; that is to say a person who performs the function of reading it on such occasions as worship in the gurdwara and at weddings. The responsibilities are ill defined, not being mentioned in the **Rahit Maryada**. Strictly speaking, there is no need or place for such a functionary in what is a lay religion but respect for the scripture requires that when it has been installed at the beginning of the day someone should attend it. In India the granthi may act as custodian of the gurdwara, in a country like Britain duties may include teaching children to read the Guru Granth Sahib and write gurmukhi. For these an honorarium may be paid. This, together with his duties would be determined by the sangat which appointed him.

Grihastha See **gristhi**.

Gristhi Punjabi form of the Sanskrit grihastha, the second, householder stage of life of the twice-born Hindu male. Sikhs reject the four ashramas, replacing them with the single one of gristhi which is open to people of any caste and through which God may ideally be realized. The Sikh ideal is that of being married and having a family, earning one's living by honest socially useful employment, serving one's fellow human beings and worshipping God. The following passage should be read as a critique of those men who left their homes to become saddhus or sannyasins and as a commendation of the gristhi life, not as a

71

suggestion that it is in any way second best. It is also necessary to remember that the path of renunciation was open only to men. 'Contemplation of the True Lord brings illumination which enables one to live detached in the midst of evil. Such is the distinctive greatness of the True Guru through whose grace and guidance salvation may be attained even though one be surrounded by one's wife and children' (AG 661).

Gurbānī The speech (bani) of the Gurus, that is the compositions of the first five and ninth Gurus and those of Guru Gobind Singh. However, the term, or the word bani, is commonly used to refer to any hymns found in the Guru Granth Sahib.

Gurbilās Literally 'the Guru's pleasure'. There are two compositions of this name, *Gurbilas Padshai Chhemi*, pertaining to Guru Hargobind, and *Gurbilas Dasvi Padshai*, relating to Guru Gobind Singh. The first dates from the period 1833 – 43 and was composed by Bhai Gurmukh Singh of Akalbunga and Bhai Darbara Singh of Amritsar; the second is actually the earlier of the two, dating from about 1795. Its author was Bhai Sukha Singh of Anandpur.

The purpose of such pseudonimous writings was presumably to remind Sikhs of truths which the authors thought they were neglecting or to deal with matters of contemporary concern which the Gurus had not actually addressed and claim that the words and instructions were those of the Gurus. Thus Guru Hargobind is said to have decreed that only a man well-versed in the gurbani should be appointed to look after a gurdwara, and that he should be of good character so that he can set a good example. He also admonished his daughter, Bibi Viro, to respect her husband's parents and family, and not feel proud of her own parentage. In the second, Guru Gobind Singh says that God ordained him to create the Khalsa, that any Sikh who abandons the rahit (code of conduct), is like an ass in the skin of a lion, and that no keshdhari Sikh should ever enter his presence unarmed. 'A Sikh without arms is like a sheep, anyone can catch him by the ears.'

Gurdās, Bhāī (1551 – 1637) The nephew of Guru Amar Das being the son of his younger brother. He was a competent expositor of the teachings of the Gurus and worked for some time as a missionary in Agra. He helped Guru Arjan compile the Adi Granth and is reputed to have met the Emperor Akbar in 1605 and assured him that the Sikh scripture contained nothing derogatory to Islam. After the martyrdom of Guru Arjan and again when Guru Hargobind was a prisoner in the Gwalior fort, he and Bahi Buddha were among the elders of the community who looked after the affairs of the Panth. He remained celebate and died at the village of Goindwal where he was born. His thirty-nine vars are of considerable historical and theological importance. They are regarded as the key to understanding Sikhism and are approved for reading in gurdwaras. Bhai Gurdas might be described as the first Sikh theologian.

Gurdwārā The name given to the place of Sikh worship, literally the doorway to the Guru. It is often described as the Sikh temple but strictly speaking the term is as inappropriate as 'Sikh church' or 'Sikh mosque' would be. Any suitable building or room in a domestic dwelling may be a gurdwara, the only requirement being that it contains a copy of the Guru Granth Sahib which may be treated with due respect. (It would not be installed in a room where people might be passing to and fro above it while it was in use, for example.) Gurdwaras known as historical through association with one of the Gurus are managed by the **Shromani Gurdwara Parbandhak Committee**, the rest are managed by committees elected by members of the sangat.

Before the time of the sixth Guru places of Sikh worship were called dharmsalas.

Gurdwaras Act 1925 The agitation of the late nineteenth century known as the **Singh Sabha** movement, culminated in a demand for the control of gurdwaras. Many of these were in the ownership or custody of people who disregarded the code of discipline associated with the **Khalsa**. Clearly the efforts of the reformers would be of no avail if Sikh places or worship and the activities which took place inside them were unaffected. After years of agitiation control of the gurdwaras of the Punjab was given to a newly-created body, the **Shromani Gurdwara Parbandhak Committee**, under the Sikh Gurdwaras Act, passed by the Punjab government in 1925. The committee had been set up in 1920 but was now given official recognition. The movement for gurdwara reform also had the important effect of developing panthic cohesion.

Gurmat This is the term generally used by Sikhs for what in English is called Sikhism. It means the teaching of the Guru but includes the disciplinary code known as the **Rahit Maryada** as well as scriptual doctrines.

Gurmattā A decision affecting the whole Sikh community. The Rahit Maryada defines the areas which may be covered by a gurmatta as 'subjects calculated to clarify and support the fundamental principles of Sikhism, such as safeguarding the position of the Gurus and the Guru Granth Sahib, purity of ritual, and panthic organization'. Political, educational and social matters may also be dealt with at panthic meetings but on these only resolutions, mattas, may be passed. These are not as sacred or inviolable as gurmattas.

A gurmatta may only be passed by the Sarbat Khalsa, that is a properly constituted assembly of the Panth which has been publicly announced and to which they have been summoned. In this way it resembles the gatherings of Sikhs in the presence of the human Gurus at Hola Mohalla, Baisakhi, and Diwali, at which such decisions were often made, though, of course, it must be held in the presence of the Guru Granth Sahib. In 1805 Maharaja Ranjit Singh abolished assemblies of the Sarbat Khalsa for this purpose, but the practice has recently been re-established.

Gurmukh Someone who has become God-oriented and God-filled instead of self-centred (manmukh), and so has attained spiritual liberation.

Gurmukhī The written form of Punjabi used in the Sikh scriptures and in India. (In Pakistan the Urdu script is used for writing Punjabi.) It comprises thirty-five letters plus a number of accents. The literal meaning of the word, from the mouth of the Guru, is a reminder that the alphabet, in its present form, is the product of the Sikh Gurus. Guru Nanak composed an acrostic using the letters of the alphabet but it was his successor, Guru Angad, who finalized it while all the Gurus popularized it by using it, rather than the Devanagri script, in all their writings. The consequence was the encouragement of literacy in the Punjab, as well as the development of Punjabi literature. It has also resulted in Punjabi and Gurmukhi being given the status of a sacred language by some Sikhs.

Gurpurb The festival celebrated on the anniversary of the birth or death of a Guru. Certain other occasions such as the anniversary of the installation of the Adi Granth in 1604, or the deaths of the sons of the tenth Guru may also be included. The birthdays of Guru Nanak and Guru Gobind Singh and the martyrdom of Guru Arjan are observed universally, others tend only to be celebrated locally unless it is the centennial of an event. In India and some other countries the Guru Granth Sahib is carried in procession, led by the panj piare; this is known as nagar kirtan or a jalous, but an **akhand path** is the main feature of the celebration. A general invitation to langar may be extended in villages and people passing gurdwaras may find themselves being offered oranges or other kinds of fruit.

Gursikh A term of respect used of someone who is deeply and sincerely devoted to the service of the Guru.

Gurū One of the most important words in Sikhism, it has a number of related meanings. First, it refers to God. The way in which **Akal Purukh**, the Being Beyond Time, enters the temporal dimension is as Guru. This means that God is the divine preceptor whose word infuses enlightenment. Sometimes the

75

term **Sat Guru** is used to describe this revelatory aspect of God. The fifth Guru declared, 'The True Guru is God. Do not believe that God is in the form of a man' (AG895).

Guru Arjan is also prepared to use sectarian names of the Guru though at the same time affirming that the Guru is the supreme being, Brahman. 'My Guru is Parbrahman, my Guru is Gobind . . . Bhagvan, Allekh and Abekh' (AG 964).

The above quotations may reject the concept of **avatar** and the claims of human Gurus to have divine qualities but they also assert the principle that divine revelation may be found in Hinduism and Islam, the forms of religion of which the Sikh Gurus had first-hand experience.

Secondly, the word is used of the ten human Gurus. Though only seven of them, including Guru Gobind Singh, were men through whom the **gurbani** was revealed, all are regarded as being of equal standing as messengers of God. 'The same is the divine light, the same is the life form. The king has merely changed the body' (AG 966), is the way that bards at the court of Guru Arjan expressed it.

The Sikh Gurus are, naturally, highly respected. It is often said that their birth was non-karmic, that is that they were in a state of bliss in the presence of God and were born in obedience to the divine will and not as a consequence of karma. However, they are not objects of worship, their pictures should never be placed in such a position in the gurdwara that people bowing towards the Guru Granth Sahib, bow accidentally towards them.

The third use of the word Guru is in the expression Guru Granth Sahib, the phrase used to refer to the sacred scripture of the Sikhs. When he installed it as Guru, just before his death, the tenth Guru was, among other things acknowledging that it was the message, the word given to him and his predecessors, that was the Guru. By including the compositions of Hindus and Muslims in the collection of sacred writings, Sikhism also expresses the belief that revelation is not confined to the utterances of the human Gurus.

Less attention is given to the fourth aspect of guruship, the Guru Panth, the Sikh community which lives according to the teachings of the scriptures and is inspired by them. When it deliberates upon spiritual issues in the presence of the Guru Granth Sahib it reaches decisions called gurmatta. (N.B. Each human Guru is covered by a separate entry.)

Gurū Granth Sāhib The principal scripture of the Sikhs which may be seen installed in all gurdwaras and is essentially present and the focus of attention on almost all ceremonial and ritual occasions. The origins of the book go back as far as Guru Nanak. Not only was he inspired to compose shabads but there is also the possibility that he began to collect them before his death. It is clear too that he knew at least some of the bhagat bani; for example, on page 729 is his comment on a verse of Sheikh Farid's found on page 794 — presumably they existed side by side in some collections but were separated by Guru Arjan when he compiled the Adi Granth in 1604. However, the chief credit for assembling the bani of Guru Nanak belongs to his successor, Guru Angad. By the time of the fifth Guru a number of collections existed and there is evidence that spurious material was being circulated to denigrate the Gurus, undermine the Panth, and support the claims of rivals like the Guru's own brother. There was a very real need for an authoritative compilation.

Guru Arjan was not content simply to gather together authentic material, he also deliberately arranged it according to Indian ragas, in thirty-one sections. On each of these he imposed an order, first the works of Guru Nanak and his successors, then the bani of the **bhagats**, with **Kabir** first, then **Sheikh Farid**, followed by **Namdev** and **Ravidas**. Not all the Gurus or bhagats are represented in each section. The few works of the other fourteen bhagats, thirty-six in all, are scattered throughout the volume. The contents of the scripture are, without exception, poetical. Narrative elements of the lives of the Gurus occur in

77

non-canonical literature known as janam sakhis. Various languages and Indian dialects were used by the authors of the bani but all are written in the gurmukhi script.

Printed copies of the Guru Granth Sahib were produced in the latter quarter of the nineteenth century and eventually installed in gurdwaras though there was initial resistance to their replacing handwritten volumes. The printed versions are all of uniform length, being 1430 pages long. It is common practice, therefore, to cite only the page when giving reference to quotations from the scripture, though many writers still alude to the rag and the subsection from which the passage has been taken.

On page 1429 are some words of Guru Arjan's which might be regarded as summing up the whole purpose of the scripture. The passage is called Mundavani, The Seal. It reads as follows: 'In the platter are placed three things: truth, contentment and meditation. The nectar name of the Lord, the support of all has also been put on it. Whoever eats this food, whoever relishes it, is emancipated. This cannot be forsaken so keep it always enshrined in your mind. Falling down at the Lord's feet the dark world ocean is crossed. O Nanak, everything is an extension of the Lord'.

Ritually, the Guru Granth Sahib is treated like a living Guru in many respects, for that is, in effect, what it is. It is taken in procession in the morning (parkash karna), from its resting place, to the manji sahib upon which it is installed under a canopy (chanani). An attendant stands by it holding a chauri, an emblem of authority, in the hand and waving it occasionally over the book, worshippers prostrate themselves in front of it on entering its presence, and at night it is ceremonially returned to its resting place in procession (sukh asan). Even more significantly, its advice is taken by opening it at random and reading the first complete verse on the left hand page; this is known as taking the vak. Continuous or interrupted readings of the scripture (akhand paths or sidharan paths), are necessary accompaniments to all Sikh festivals and life-cycle rituals.

Gutkā   A small anthology of daily and occasional prayers. It may also contain popular hymns for congregational singing. It is treated with considerable respect, often being wrapped in a cloth, kept on a high shelf above other books, and only handled after the hands have been washed. (See also **nitnem**.)

Hargobind, Guru   (born 14 June 1595, Guru 25 May 1606 to 3 March 1644) At the birth of his only son Guru Arjan composed the following verse: 'The Sat Guru has sent the child, the long-lived child has been born by destiny. When he came and acquired an abode in the womb, his mother's heart became glad. The son, the saint of the world lord (Govind) is born' (AG 396).

This was a time when Sikh aspirations were perhaps at their highest. The Panth was expanding, the Emperor, Akbar, was tolerant and open minded, he and the fifth Guru had actually held a meeting. The name Gobind may indicate the Guru's hopes for the future. However, in 1605 Akbar died, his successor had Guru Arjan executed, and the young sixth Guru found himself leading the Sikhs in a new and unexpected situation. He symbolically wore two swords, representing temporal and spiritual authority, as part of his regalia, and kept a standing army. One of his titles was Sacha Padshah, True Emperor, which was among those used by Mughal emperors. Guru Ram Das was addressed by this name but now, with the Guru holding court and using ambassadors, it must have assumed a new significance. Relations with the two emperors who were his overlords varied. He went hunting with Jehangir, though he also spent a short time in the fort at Gwalior as his prisoner. He was involved in the opposition to Shah Jehan's policy of demolishing Hindu and Sikh places of worship, and his laws dissolving mixed marriages. Towards the end of his life he established a base at Kiratpur in the Shivalik hills which became a focus for the disaffected. The first official use of military force by Sikhs probably belongs to this period. Perhaps because of the breaks with tradition which Guru Hargobind made, his comtemporary Bhai Gurdas wrote: 'Former Gurus have consolation sitting on a manji, the present one keeps dogs and hunts. They would compose shabads, listen to them and join in the singing; the present Guru does not compose, listen or sing. His companions are not Sikhs. He has wicked and bad men as his guides' (Var 26).

Guru Hargobind built gurdwaras at places associated with his predecessors and repaired others. It may be that it was during his lifetime that the name gurdwara was first used of Sikh places or worship, though the earlier name, dharmsala, persisted in use until the twentieth century and may still be used in villages today.

(The spelling Hargovind is also found and sometimes the two parts of the Guru's name are separated.)

Har Krishan, Gurū   (born 7 July 1656, Guru 7 October 1661 to 30 March 1664) Sometimes called the boy Guru, the eighth, younger son of Guru Har Rai, had to contend with hostility and suspicion from the new Mughal Emperor, Aurangzeb, during his brief period as Guru. His elder brother, Ram Rai, kept at the imperial court, was put forward as a rival, though without success. The Guru was summoned to Delhi so that the Emperor might decide who should lead the Sikhs. While under house arrest Guru Har Krishan contracted smallpox and died, nominating 'Baba Bakale' as successor, (Guru Tegh Bahadur, his uncle, who lived in Bakala). Gurdwara Bangla Sahib stands at the place where the young Guru died. Educational establishments are often named after him. (The spelling Harkrishan and Har Krishen are also used.)

Harmandir Sāhib   See **Darbār Sāhib**.

Har Rāi, Gurū   (Born 30 January 1630, Guru 8 March, 1644 to 6 October 1661) Although he continued to maintain a court and did not compose shabads, the seventh Guru seems to have reverted to the ways of the first five rather than that of his father. He had a reputation for knowledge of herbal medicines and supplied a remedy for an illness of the son of Emperor Shah

Jehan. He incurred the suspicion of the Emperor Auranzeb for supporting his rival, Prince Dara, in a war of succession, and was summond to the Mughal court. He sent his son instead and the young man, Ram Rai, was used by the Emperor in an attempt to create disloyalty among the Sikhs.

Haṭha Yoga A form of tantric yoga the origins of which may lie in Mahayana Buddhism. Its literal meaning is the yoga of force because of the physically demanding nature of the processes and postures used in realizing it. Through these the adept acquires great energy and power. Guru Nanak especially, but also his successors, made many references to these yogis in their compositions for a number of reasons; they were ubiquitous throughout north India, they were popular in their appeal reaching, unlike Brahminism, people of low caste, and in some respects their monotheism and opposition to caste meant that there was an affinity between the teachings of Sikhs and Naths, as they are often called. The word means 'Master' (of yogic power). Guru Nanak frequently used Nath terminology.

There were also considerable differences. The Naths placed considerable emphasis upon physical effort; Guru Nanak believed that the goal of spiritual liberation could be reached without it and that often these practices became ostentatious ends in themselves. Naths were ascetics and lived apart from the rest of society. This was against the Sikh view that spiritual realization takes place in the context of the family and the service of humanity. The Naths were also charged with being parasites and hypocrites, preying upon the superstitions and fears of villagers.

The common word which is used in the Guru Granth Sahib to refer to the practitioners of hatha yoga is quite simply 'yogis' but many other terms are also found, Siddhas, Gorakhnathis, 'split-eared ones) ('Kanphata Yogis'), as well as Naths.

The importance which Guru Nanak attached to refuting the yogis was such that one of his compositions is cast in the form of a disputation (gosht) with them. Known as Siddha Gosht it is found on pages 937 to 943 of the Guru Granth Sahib. From it comes the following passage which invites the yogi to put away his elaborate rituals and distinctive dress and, instead, assume the garment of God's Name and the habit of self-control: 'Continually enshrine the name of God in your mind. Make the renunciation of self and attachment be your earrings. Disgard lust, wrath and pride, and, by the guru's instruction, you will receive sublime wisdom. Behold the Lord who is all-pervading, make him your patched coat and begging bowl and he will ferry you across (the world-ocean). Let control of your body be your asana and mind-control your loin cloth' (AG 939).

Guru Nanak may not have made a comment quite as acerbic as that of Kabir, 'A pig is worth more than a shakta, for it keeps the village clean', but there is no doubt that he shared the view that they were pernicious as well as preachers of a message of false hope.

Haumai Human beings in their natural, as opposed to their liberated form, are subject to the impulse of haumai. It is difficult to define the meaning of the term as used by Guru Nanak but a beginning might be made by noting that the literal meaning is 'I-I', hau-main. The word is used in both a spiritual and ethical sense so that 'pride' and 'self-centredness' may sometimes be used as appropriate translations.

The consequence of haumai is that one is self-willed (manmukh) as opposed to being obedient to the Word of the Sat Guru (gurmukh). The consequence is rebirth. Haumai is part of God's creation since nothing exists unless God wills it to: 'God created the world and also invested it with haumai; one's mind is purged only if one enshrines the Word in the mind' (AG 1010).

It has some purpose and value: 'Under the compulsion of haumai man comes and goes, is born and dies, gives and takes, earns and loses, speaks truth and lies, smears himself with evil and washes himself of it' (AG 466).

It may prompt a person to good actions, but the motive is always selfish and therefore haumai is a chain binding humans to the cycle of rebirth. Guru Nanak continues, 'When haumai is banished then access to the door (of liberation) is gained; without knowledge of God there is only argument and wrangling; destiny is written by God's Order (hukam).'

The juxtaposition of haumai and hukam is not accidental, humanity is expected to transcend its natural state and live according to God's will.

If anyone comprehends the hukam his haumai is purged (AG 1). Haumai is a veil of falsehood, as the poet Bhai Vir Singh put it, which prevents us from attaining to the Truth. The way to live according to Truth is be practising **Nam Simran**.

When one is imbued with Nam, haumai ceases to exist (AG 941).

Hazur Sahib   This gurdwara is one of the five takhts or seats of doctrinal authority. It is situated at Nander in Hyderbad, where Guru Gobind Singh died. The inner room of the gurdwara, called Angitha Sahib, is built over the place where he was cremated.

Heaven and Hell   Guru Nanak uses popular terms found in the Indian tradition, such as Svaraga and Baikunth, paradise or heaven, and even the name of the god of death, Yam. ('Man is like a fish caught in Yam's net. Without the Guru, the giver, there is no salvation' AG 934.) However, there is no reason to think that he was doing more than make use of the popular vocabulary which was familiar to his audience.

Sikhism teaches what may be called a demythologized concept of heaven, hell and the after life. Guru Arjan said: 'Baikunth is wherever God's praises are sung (AG 749) and wherever godly people live, that is Baikunth. They enshrine the lotus-feet of the Lord in their minds (AG 742). On the other hand, in the midst of a myriad joys, if one does not cherish the Lord's Name one lives as if in the depths of hell' (AG 707).

Sikhism holds to the concept of jivan mukt, liberation while in this life, and also that this has ethical obligations; bliss, Anand, is not enjoyed by separation from the world, but by living like the lotus in the pond, pure and uncontaminated. 'Heaven (Bhisatu) is not entered by mere words, deliverance comes through truthful living' (AG 141).

There is an element of judgement in Sikh thought but the emphasis is upon the present life in which the eternal destiny of a person is decided. 'One who indulges in sensuous pleasures here suffers misery hereafter' (AG 1276): 'In the hereafter one's words and deeds are scrutinized and one is brought to account for them' (AG 464), but good deeds, though important as a proper response to God's grace, do not secure ultimate and eternal bliss: 'Through your Name the soul (man) finds total bliss. Without the Name one goes bound to the city of Yam.'

There are many passages in the bani of Guru Nanak which indicate acceptance of the Hindu belief in rebirth, and the effects of karma; however, such ideas are not the one's which concern him ultimately. His preoccupation was with enabling his listeners to become one with God and so escape the death of separation which awaited them if they persisted in duality.

Holā Mohallā In 1680 Guru Gobind Singh summoned his followers to appear in his presence at Anandpur. He organized a mock battle, archery and wrestling contests, and also music and poetry competitions. This mela was intended to wean Sikhs away from the Hindu celebration of Holi and has become an established part of the Sikh calendar though the main celebration is still held at Anandpur. It culminates in a procession headed by the nishan sahibs of the gurdwaras of the region.

Hukam In the Japji, after affirming that God is Truth, Guru Nanak asked, 'How is Truth to be attained?' (AG 1). The answer he gave is, 'Submit to the hukam, walk in its way'. Hukam is an Arabic word meaning Divine Order. Creation is the product of this Order, and so is the natural human condition. 'All are subject to God's Order, nothing lies outside it' (AG 1).

This is expanded in the following verse: 'When you are true everything that flows from you is true; nothing, nothing at all is false. Talking, seeing, uttering, walking, living, and dying, are

84

all from you. Nanak, the True Lord creates by his Order, and keeps all things in his order' (AG 145).

When Guru Nanak said, 'All are engaged in obeying the hukam' (AG 8) he was exempting human beings in their natural state; they may be subject to it ultimately, but they choose to follow their own path being dominated by self-will (haumai).

Sometimes hukam is translated as 'God's will'; this may be acceptable so long as it is realized that the Sikh emphasis is upon consistency and orderliness. God is compassionate, but not a whimsical Being whose mind is changeable and purpose vacillating. Liberation comes, not from changing God but from a change or orientation in the one who seeks it.

Rahai, or reza, the pleasure or will of God, a term used especially by Sufis, is also used by Guru Nanak, but less frequently. It tends to be used to refer to the spirit of dedication with which one does one's duty.

Hukam Nāmā This Persian word means a letter containing a royal command. It is used in Sikhism to refer to instructions issued by the Sikh Gurus, the wives of Guru Gobind Singh, Banda Bahadur, and, later and in the present day, the jathedars of the five takhts. Whoever is actually responsible for issuing them, they are regarded as the commands of the Guru and are binding upon the whole Panth.

The need for hukam namas arose as the Sikh community grew in size and became widespread in its geographical distribution. Matters which Guru Nanak might have dealt with verbally in the course of giving darshan now had to be committed to paper. Also, with the development of the Panth, they became more complex. In the nineteenth century one was issued condemning Maharaja Ranjit Singh for a moral lapse and requiring him to submit to a public flogging to demonstrate his repentance. After the destruction of the Akal Takht during Operation Blue Star in 1984, Baba Santa Singh Nihang, chief of the Buddha Dal with other Sikhs, was declared religiously and socially ostracized for disregarding a hukam nama forbidding them from undertaking the work.

Hukam namas may take the form of exhortations and commendations, or prohibitions. They may relate to individuals or to the Panth as a whole.

Ik Oaṅkār   This is one of the two most used Sikh symbols, the other being the **khanda**. It is formed from the figure one and the word 'oankar' which are found at the beginning of the **Mul mantra** and may often be seen on the front of the chanani or takht above the Guru Granth Sahib. The symbol reminds the Sikh of the whole content of the Mul mantra but is also an affirmation in its own right of the belief that God is one. It corresponds to the word Om in Hinduism.

Infanticide   A practice condemned by the Gurus, though it has sometimes been practised by Sikhs when the baby is a girl or physically deformed.

Jaidev   A poet who lived in the twelfth century and was employed at the court of Lakshman Sen, King of Bengal. Famous as the author of the Sanskrit poem *Gita Govinda*. Two of his compositions in Hindu are in the Guru Granth Sahib.

Jalāu, jalōus   An outdoor procession led by the Guru Granth Sahib and the **panj piare** as part of a celebration, especially a **gurpurb**. May be used synonymously with **nagar kirtan**. Literally, a display of splendour and in this sense used of an exhibition of the treasures of the Darbar Sahib (Golden Temple) in Amritsar.

Janam Sākhī   A hagiographic account of the life of Guru Nanak, literally a 'life story'. There are several janam sakhis related to a number of different traditions, not all of them well disposed towards the main stream of orthodoxy represented by the succession of Gurus. One, for example, known as the Miharban Janam Sakhi after its supposed author Sodhi Miharban, is regarded as having been produced to support the ideas and leadership claims of Prithi Chand, eldest son of Guru Ram Das, against his younger brother, Arjan, who became the fifth Guru.

Some Sikhs place a high value upon the janam sakhis as historical sources for the life of Guru Nanak while others see them as testimonies to the piety of the Panth during the century following his ministry, when most of them were written.

The janam sakhis present a portrait of Guru Nanak as a wise, charismatic figure who travelled widely proclaiming God's Word to a world which had forgotten it and was lost in evil and superstitious religiosity. This is often personified in a religious person, Hindu or Muslim, or someone of worldly importance, a ruler or man of property, who seeks to argue with, impress, deceive, or even harm the Guru or his constant companion, Mardana. However, the enlightenment of the Guru, and the Word are too powerful and the result is usually conversion or at least the discrediting of the opponent. Other witnesses of the event are persuaded of the truth of the divine Word and become Sikhs. Frequently there is mention of a dharmsala being built and the episode ends with Guru Nanak composing or singing a shabad relevant to the particular situation before going on his way.

Such pericopes comprise the bulk of each janam sakhis but there are usually episodes concerned with his childhood and descriptions of his death. Bala, a Hindu, features in one of the janam sakhis, which is named after him and accredited to him. No other tradition mentions him and there is a tendency nowadays to doubt his companionship of the Guru. The company of the Muslim musician, Mardana, on the other hand seems to be well attested.

The janam sakhis were used by preachers to make the presence of Guru Nanak real to congregations which had never seen or heard him. They are still used today for this purpose. Through the stories which they hear Sikhs not only enter the world of Guru Nanak but also feel that the sometimes abstract ideas of his bani, or hymns, are made more comprehensible when through being attached to incidents in his life.

Jap The devout repetition of the divine name, **Wahiguru**, a mantra, or scripture.

Japjī This shabad, traditionally regarded as the first of Guru Nanak's compositions, contains the essence of Sikh meditation. The name of the poem means 'meditation'. So important is it to Sikhs that Guru Arjan placed it at the very beginning of the Adi Granth and assigned it alone to no musical rag, presumably to draw attention to it as the supreme aid to personal meditation, but also so that no one should run the risk of being distracted from its sublime words by the interference of music. A Sikh should meditate upon the Japji every morning. It is also used in the ceremony of Khalsa initiation.

Jap Sāhib One of the most important devotional compositions of Guru Gobind Singh. It should be recited, together with the Guru's *Ten Swayyas* and *Japji* of Guru Nanak each morning. It consists of one hundred and ninety-nine brief stanzas which describe the nature and qualities of God.

Jassā Siṅgh Ālūwāliā (1718 – 1783) A famous Sikh soldier, he was brought up by the widow of Guru Gobind Singh, Mata Sundri, and eventually came to the notice of Sardar Kapur Singh, leader of the **Dal Khalsa**. In 1748 Jassa Singh was himself appointed its leader and led it from then until 1767 in the struggle against the Afghan armies of Ahmed Shah Abdali. Among his achievements was the liberation of Amritsar, 1748, the rebuilding of the Darbar Sahib, 1764, and the capture of the Red Fort in Delhi, 1783. The **Aluwalia** subcaste of Sikhs takes its name from him.

Jassā Singh Rāmgaṛhiā (1723 – 1802) Leader of the Ramgarhia misl in the Dal Khalsa established by Kapur Singh in 1748. His area of influence lay in what is now the Gurdaspur district of the Punjab. He played a prominent part in the Sikh capture of Delhi in 1783, and built the famous gurdwaras known as Sis Ganj, on the site of Guru Tegh Bahadur's martyrdom, and Rekab Ganj, where the Guru's body was cremated.

Jaṭ North Indian farmer caste dominant in the Punjab. Jats are famous for their martial spirit, egalitarianism, and the value they place upon family pride. Not all Sikhs are Jats by any means though they constitute the largest group. Many Jats are Hindus or Muslims. Though they may repudiate caste, nevertheless they regard themselves as well born and superior socially to other groups except brahmins. They are said to have originated from the locks of Shiva's hair, hence, it is said, their own tradition of wearing the hair long or uncut.

Jathā Used of a detachment of the Dal Khalsa, the term is now used of subgroups within Sikhism using a particular form of meditation or kirtan singing, and of groups of demonstrators.

Jathedār Originally this term was used of the leader of a unit of Sikh volunteers who had devoted themselves to the full-time service of the Panth. An English equivalent might be the word 'captain'. During the **Akali** movement at the turn of the twentieth century such groups achieved a prominence and importance which they had not had since the struggles of the eighteenth century against the Mughals and Afghans as they took part in the agitation for Sikh control of the gurdwaras.

Jathedar is also the title given to the appointed head of one of the Sikh **takhts,** such as the Akal Takht. He is a paid official chosen by the **Shromani Gurdwara Parbandhak Committee** to serve for an indefinite period which can be for life. He may issue **hukam namas** but only after a panthic conference. Sometimes 'high priest' is used by westerners and some Sikhs to describe him but this is misleadingly inaccurate and should be avoided. A jathedar is a lay person, like all Sikhs, and in theory any man or woman may hold the office.

Jāti A Sanskrit generic term for an endogamous caste grouping. The Punjabi word 'zat' is often used by Sikhs.

Jhatka A technical term used to describe the approved method of animal slaughter and the meat which results from it. The words

89

Sat Sri Akal should be said over the animal and then its head severed from its body by a single blow with a sharp sword or other instrument. Although this is how Sikhs may kill animals themselves there is little evidence to suggest that they will only eat meat which is jhatka. However, the eating of halal meat, that which has been slaughtered according to Islamic requirements, was expressly forbidden by Guru Gobind Singh. This was in response to the Mughal regulation that only halal meat was lawful. Bhai Kahan Singh, an influential Sikh thinker living at the turn of the twentieth century, saw no objection to killing animals by shooting them or by electric shock and eating the meat without draining the blood from it. It should be remembered that Guru Hargobind and Guru Gobind Singh both enjoyed hunting.

Jīvaṇ Mukti The Sikh belief that a person might achieve spiritual liberation during her or his lifetime and not only on death. Such people, being completely obedient to God's will would not acquire further karma but would, of course, have to exhaust that which they had already accumulated. They are said to be jivan mukt. 'Whoever enshrines God's Name in the mind is liberated when alive' (AG 412).

Ks, **Five K**s or **Pañj Kakke** The external symbols worn by Khalsa Sikhs as obligatory but by many others through choice. They are **kes**, **kangha**, **kirpan**, **kara**, and **kachh**. Sometimes symbolic meanings are given to them but such interpretations are subject to some doubt. Their primary significance is as marks of identity.

Kabīr A member of the weaver (jullaha) caste which may have become Muslim before his birth. He lived from about 1440 – 1518, though the precise dates are uncertain. He taught the oneness of God, the irrelevance of sectarian and caste differences, and the rejection of outward forms of religiosity, preferring the practice of meditation. He also taught that liberation was open to all. His teachings are consistent with those

90

of Sikhism in many respects and five hundred and forty-one of his hymns are included in the Adi Granth. This is more than the contributions of other men whose works are constitute the **bhagat bani**. Similarities between his teachings and those of Guru Nanak, and some accounts of meetings between the two men led to a suggestion that the Guru was influenced by Kabir. The janam sakhi accounts are considered unreliable and scholars agree that there is no real evidence that they did meet. It is not impossible that Guru Nanak knew the hymns of Kabir, he may well have collected the material which is now found in the Adi Granth, but kinship of thought should not be regarded as evidence of dependence.

Kabīr panthi A devotee of the religious teacher **Kabīr**.

Kachh A pair of shorts, part of the required clothing of a Khalsa Sikh either male or female. Worn as an undergarment by women and by males who have adopted western dress.

Kalyug The fourth age or kalpa of the world and the least religious. One in which righteousness and godliness will be forgotten. It is the period in which humanity is now living. 'This age is like a drawn knife, kings are butchers and righteousness has fled. In this darkest night of utter falseness the moon of truth is not visible' (AG 145). The Gurus frequently remarked upon it and described themselves as God's messengers to it.

Kāma One of the four **dharmas** or goals in the life of a twice-born Hindu. The pursuit of love or pleasure. This is regarded as acceptable to Sikhs so long as it is treated with moderation and within the moral framework provided by the householder (**gristhi**), life-style. Otherwise it degenerates into lust, one of the **vices** which Sikhs should avoid.

Kanghā The comb which members of the Khalsa are required to wear in their hair to hold the topknot of the **kes** in place.

91

Kapur Siṅgh, Nawāb A famous Sikh hero of the eighteenth century. He was born in 1697 of a Jat family. He became leader of the Sikh forces resisting Afghan and Mughal armies and organized them into the **Dal Khalsa**. In 1733 the Afghans, Zakarifa Khan, made peace with the Sikhs and bestowed the title of 'nawab' on Kapur Singh. He died in 1754.

Kara The steel bangle which members of the Khalsa are required to wear upon the wrist of the right hand. It is not an ornament like the bangles which many women wear. The kara worn by Sikh men and women should be plain and of steel not silver or gold.

Kaṛāh Parshād (Prasād) A special food, prasad, which should be prepared in an iron pan, karaha, hence the name. It is made of equal parts of wholemeal flour, sugar and ghee (clarified butter). These are prepared to the consistency of a stiff pudding. It should then be brought into the presence of the congregation where six verses from the Anand Sahib are said over it after which the person officiating at the function touches it with a kirpan. Before the food is distributed to the congregation five portions of it should be set aside for the **panj piare** and given to five members who are known to be faithful in keeping the vows made at their initiation. Every person in the congregation regardless of caste or religion, should be offered karah parshad, beginning with whoever is reading the Guru Granth Sahib. Sometimes this portion is put in a small bowl or saucer and observers think that it is being offered to the book. It is not, but the reader may delay eating it until the task is completed for fear of handling the scripture with greasy fingers. Karah parshad should be taken in cupped hands and eaten at once.

Karma The same word in Punjabi, strictly speaking 'karamu', may mean deeds or religious obligations or fate (resulting from the consequence of such actions). From the Arabic 'karam' rather than the Sanskrit root it may mean the favour or grace of God.

Guru Nanak uses it 160 times in the former sense and ten times with the latter meaning. Here our concern is with the first use of the term.

Sikhism accepts the Hindu belief in rebirth though it is not something that the Gurus defended against the Muslim idea that the soul, or jiva, inhabits only one body. They were far more concerned with enabling people to attain spiritual liberation. However, there is strong denunciation in their compositions of any suggestions that ritual acts of any kind can secure a better rebirth or are of help to those already dead. With typical wit Guru nanak said: 'Rice balls are offered partly to the gods, and partly to ancestors. But actually it is the brahmin who kneeds and eats all of them! Seek, therefore the rice balls of God's grace which are of inexhausible efficacy' (AG 358). 'Those who know the grace (karma) of God realise that rituals (karma) are futile' (AG 470).

It is morally good and bad deeds which determine the future lives of human beings but even these have limited value; at the beginning of his most famous composition, the Japji, Guru Nanak affirmed: 'Good actions may procure a better life, but liberation, (mukti), comes only through grace' (AG 2). 'It is by dwelling on God's Name that one avoids going to Hell' (AG 465).

There is no acceptance of a law of karma in any sense which suggests inevitability or the sufficiency of human effort.

Kār Sevā A composite expression derived from kar meaning work and seva, service. It is used of any voluntary work carried out for religious purposes but especially the building of gurdwaras which traditionally has been undertaken by Sikhs themselves rather than by paid, outside contractors. The term is also used in a particular sense to refer to the removal of silt from the sarovar of the **Darbar Sahib** every fifty years, the first taking place in 1923. Although this was undertaken in 1973 in accordance with the normal schedule, because of the desecration of the pool during Operation Blue Star, a special kar sava took place in 1985.

On such occasions Sikhs in their thousands, from all walks of life, using every means of transport, and on foot, converge on the Darbar Sahib, Golden Temple, eager to participate in an activity which usually occurs only once in a lifetime.

Kartā Purukh One of the names of God, who is frequently described as the Creator by Guru Nanak. God is the first and only cause of everything that exists. There is no room in Sikh thought for the independent origination of the world, or any kind of dualism. 'God, the One, creates and performs all. Brahma, Vishnu, and Shiva, are only forms of the Creator' (AG 908). 'The One who builds, demolishes as well, for there is no other' (AG 934).

Kartārpur There are two places of this name in the history of Sikhism. The first 'city of the creator' was a small town founded by Guru Nanak on the right bank of the river Ravi in what is now Pakistan. It was here that the Guru settled with his family after spending twenty years in travelling throughout the eastern world from Sri Lanka to Tibet and Burma to Mecca. Here the ideal Sikh community was established. To paraphrase the words of Bhai Gurdas (Var 1), the Guru ascended his gaddi (seat of authority and teaching) and preached dharma. He uttered words of enlightenment and initiated the Sikh practice which still exists of rising early, at amrit vela (the period before dawn), bathing, and reciting the Japji. During the day his followers worked, in the evening they assembled to listen to his preaching and, before going to rest sang Sodar and Arati, two of his compositions. It was there that Guru Nanak died.

The other town of this name was founded by Guru Arjan in 1596 and is situated in India, near Jullunder. The original copy of the Adi Granth is kept there in a gurdwara called Shish Mahal.

Kathā An exposition of Sikh teachings based on the Guru Granth Sahib or Dasam Granth. The speaker may also use the compositions of Bhai Gurdas or Bhai Nandlal and material from

Sikh history to illustrate the discourse, but the purpose should be to promote the spirituality of the congregation. References to other religions and their sacred books may be made but only in a spirit of respect for them. No talk which contradicts the tenets of Sikhism may be given in a gurdwara.

Kes The uncut hair which a Khalsa Sikh must keep. The prohibition against cutting the hair applies to the whole body, not only the scalp of the head.

Kesdhāri A Sikh man or woman who observes the prohibition against cutting the hair. Such a person should not be confused with an **amritdhari** Sikh who has undergone the amrit initiation ceremony and is required to keep all the five Ks and the initiation vows.

Keshgaṛh Sāhib A gurdwara in the town of Anandpur Sahib on the site of Baisakhi assembly of 1699 where the first amrit initiation ceremony took place. Some of the weapons of Guru Gobind Singh are kept in it; especially important is the khanda which he used in preparing the amrit. The present building dates from the nineteen forties.

Keskī A head-covering worn between the hair and the turban by some Sikhs, or instead of it by some sportsmen, and by some boys before they begin to wear the turban. Occasionally worn as a small turban by women under the chunni, headscarf, especially members of the **Akhand Kirtani Jatha**.

Khālistān The land of the pure or, according to some aspirants, the land where the **Khalsa** rules. This would embrace not only the present Indian state of the Punjab, but also other territory that was under the rule of Maharaja **Ranjit Singh**, and an outlet to the Indian Ocean. During the agitations of the 1970s and 1980s for greater home rule in the Punjab, demands have sometimes been made for a separate Sikh state independent of the Indian republic, to be called Khalistan.

95

During the independence negotiations in 1946, when the partition of India was being discussed (a solution which Sikhs strongly opposed), Sardar Baldev Singh used the word 'Khalistan' to describe an area where Sikhs would be in a dominant position. Use of the term was revived in the late 1970s when a minority of Sikhs began to agitate for independence. (Baldev Singh became first defence minister of India.)

Khālsā The community of amritdhari, initiated Sikhs, founded by Guru Gobind Singh in an impressive ceremony at Anandpur in 1699, the word means 'pure' but also refers to the land which was under the personal and direct control of a ruler. Both these meanings are significant in understanding the motives of the Guru in establishing the new Sikh institution. He was seeking to break the power of the masands, regional supervisors of the collection of tithes. They had been appointed by earlier Gurus but by now were almost independent. Guru Gobind Singh abolished them and, through the Khalsa, exercised his authority as Guru. He also gave the Khalsa distinguishing marks of identity, the five Ks, and a code of conduct which set them apart from other groups and required them to live pure lives.

Of the Khalsa Guru Gobind Singh said, 'The Khalsa is my other self, in it I live and move and have my being.' However, conscious of human fallibility, he also warned, 'So long as the Khalsa remains distinct I will confer glory on it. When it takes to the practices of Brahminism I shall no longer trust it.' Although Sikhs believe that the Guru is mystically present in the Khalsa Panth there is no place for thinking it to be infallible.

Membership of the Khalsa is effected by the initiation rite known as **amritsanskar**, introduced by Guru Gobind Singh in 1699.

Khaṇḍā A double-edged sword. It is also the name of the emblem which has a khanda in the centre surrounded by a circle called a chakkar and supported by two kirpans which extend to the right and left of it. This symbol of Sikhism may be seen on the flag of the gurdwara, the palki above the Guru Granth Sahib, worn on ties or as lapel badges.

Each of the three different weapons which make up the khanda has a symbolic meaning. The khanda itself is a sword with two blades which must be equally honed, otherwise its balance would be affected and it would be useless; it symbolizes the need for the amritdhari Sikh to be a saint-soldier. The kirpans are reminiscent of Guru Arjan's injunction to his son, Guru Hargobind, to wear two swords, one of piri, spiritual power, and the other, miri, of temporal authority. The chakkar, an extremely ancient Indian symbol, speaks of the oneness of God, the unity of humanity — undivided by caste or sex distinctions, and the nature of God as described in the **Mul Mantra**.

Khaṇḍe di Pahul See **amritsanskār**.

Khaṇḍe Ka Amrit One of the names given to the Sikh initiation rite. See **amritsanskār**.

Khatrī The mercantile caste to which the Sikh Gurus belonged. Regarded by Sikhs to be of the kshatria varna.

Kīratpur A town on the banks of the river Sutlej not far from Anandpur. It was founded by Guru Hargobind who died there. The next two Gurus were both anointed there. Guru Har Rai died there and the ashes of Guru Har Krishan were also immersed in the river there. It has become popular for Sikhs to follow this example. Some Sikhs living out of India also send the ashes of relatives to Kiratpur.

Kirpān A sword with curved blade, or a knife of similar shape. It is part of the required uniform of a khalsa Sikh. Sometimes it is described as a 'dagger' but this is a term which many Sikhs regard as inappropriate.

Kīrtan A musical rendering of the gurbani, the congregational singing of compositions from the Guru Granth Sahib, Dasam

Granth, Bhai Gurdas, or Bhai Nandlal. These are often accompanied by instruments but this is not essential. The ragis (musicians) who do perform kirtan should be Sikhs according to the **Rahit Maryada** but the Muslim descendants of **Mardana** still perform kirtan in gurdwaras.

Care must be taken to ensure that the words are clearly audible as it is the message not the music which is of primary importance. The word kirtan comes from 'kirti', praise of God.

Kirtan Sohila A brief selection of verses from the Guru Granth Sahib which should be recited at night before retiring to bed. The second line of the first hymn contains the word 'Sohila', 'Sing to his glory'. These passages are also used at funerals.

Kshatriya The second group in the varna (caste) system of Hinduism. Its traditional occupation was that of warrior. The caste grouping to which the ten Gurus belonged, the khatris, claimed kshatriya status, as the name indicates.

Kukas See **Namdhari**.

Kurahts The vows of abstinence which a Sikh makes during initiation into the **Khalsa**. These are: not to remove body hair; not to eat meat slaughtered and prepared for eating according to Islamic practice, (i.e. halal meat); adultery; the use of tobacco. The breaking of any of these rules of discipline necessitates reinitiation. One who infringes the code is known as a patit, apostate.

Langar One of the most important and fundamental Sikh institutions, that of taking food together when visiting a gurdwara. The term, which literally means 'anchor', refers both to the meal and to the place where it is prepared and served. A basic tenet* of Sikhism, proclaimed by Guru Nanak, and endorsed by all his successors, is the rejection of caste distinctions. Langar is a practical way of demonstrating this, for in Hindu society

98

* principle /precept.

commensality has often been confined to one's own caste or jati group.

Guru Nanak first established the practice of langar when he settled at Kartarpur, at the end of his period of missionary activity. By the time of Guru Amar Das it had become a requirement that all visitors should take langar before receiving his darshan. It is recorded that the Emperor Akbar and the Raja of Haripur were among those who did so. Today, in countries such as England, where worship (diwan), has become formalized beginning and ending at a set time, langar follows the service; in India, certainly at major gurdwaras, langar, like worship is ongoing throughout the day, though at **gurpurbs** it usually concludes the celebrations.

The form which langar takes varies with geography. Outdoors, sitting on the ground, possibly eating off disposable leaf plates, is usual in Indian and similar climates. Where a floor has been purposely made earth or concrete may be used, but if of earth it should never be smeared with cow-dung.

The food used at langar may be contributed by families to mark special occasions, such as a birth or marriage, or by the gurdwara committee from its common fund. At harvest time it is customary for farmers to donate sacks of grain to their village gurdwara and often to the Darbar Sahib. Any Sikh should be permitted to offer, prepare, or serve food, regardless of sex or caste. What is provided should be simple, not ostentatious, and only vegetarian, to cause no one offence. The place of langar is now largely symbolic but there are still occasions when the free distribution of food is organized to meet the needs of refugees, disaster victims or other people in need, regardless of religious belief. However, sight should not be lost of its primary purpose, the assertion of social equality.

Lāvān During a marriage ceremony the couple circum-ambulates the Guru Granth Sahib four times. This is called lavan, circling, in Punjabi. The word is also the name give to a four-stanza composition of Guru Ram Das, found on pages 773

99

and 774 of the scripture and which is read during the lavan. The verses commend the marriage union which is being embarked upon, but also stress spiritual unity with God. The first describes the householder's life focused on the Guru's word, as divinely ordained. The second affirms that the union has been brought about by God. The third speaks of their membership of the sangat in which God's praises are sung. During the final round they are congratulated on attaining their heart's desire, union with God.

It is said that lavan was composed for the wedding of one of the relatives of the Guru. For many years, until 1909, when the Anand Marriage Act was passed, the Sikhs were not allowed to practise their own ceremony of Anand Karaj. When they were, the presence of the Guru Granth Sahib, and the reading of lavan, became its central, and only necessary features.

Lohri This is a popular north Indian festival which occurs on the eve of Maghar Sangrant, the day when the sun enters Capricorn (about 12 January). The Gurus rejected the notion of auspicious days but some Sikhs do observe the festival or enjoy the bonfires lit by their Hindu neighbours. More important for Sikhs is the Maghi fair which takes place on the following day at Muktsar. This mela commemorates the battle of Muktsar fought by Guru Gobind Singh's army at Ishasar in district Ferozepur. Forty men, who had previously deserted the guru, decided to rejoin him and on their way encountered a Mughal force. In the ensuing skirmish the Sikhs were killed. The Guru described them as 'liberated ones', mukti, hence the name which the town now bears.

A few days before the actual celebration of the festival, children start collecting fuel for the bonfires and money to buy fireworks, going from door to door. They make a special point of going to homes where a child has been born or someone has been married during the year since the last Lohri festival.

Mahala Ordinarily the word is used to refer to a district of a town or to a bride. It is used in the Guru Granth Sahib to indicate

100

the authorship of a composition by one of the Gurus, each of whom used the name Nanak to demonstrate the unity of the teachings. These were not ascribed to Gurus by name but by number when Guru Arjan made his compilation. So, for example, after a work by Guru Angad will come 'Mahala 2'. This was in accord with the sectional division of the book which the fifth Guru decided to adopt, and also the concept of the Gurus being the brides of God, that is faithful transmitters of the divine message.

Mahant The term is used by Sikhs to refer to the men who administered or had the custody of gurdwaras prior to the passing of the Gurdwaras Act of 1925. During the troubles of the eighteenth century gurdwaras had often passed into the hands of Sikhs who did not observe the outward Sikh form and thereby avoided persecution. In the nineteenth century their virtual ownership of these religious premises was recognized legally by the British. Eventually agitation for the removal of the mahants and the transfer of ownership and management to the Sikhs themselves was mounted, which culminated in the passing of the Act mentioned above, and the establishment of the **Shromani Gurdwara Parbandhak Committee** to be responsible for gurdwaras in Punjab.

Main ul Mulk Ruler of the Punjab from 1748 to 1753 as a vassal of Ahmed Shah Abdali of Afghanistan. Better known as Mir Mannu. He is infamous as one who attempted the extermination of the Sikhs, so much so that they composed the following verse: 'Mannu is our sickle, to him we are weeds. As he thins us out we doubly, doubly seed.'

Mājhā Literally 'middle'. That part of the Punjab which lies between the Beas and Ravi rivers.

Mālā A necklace, wreath, or garland, but most commonly an aid to prayer or meditation. The mala used by Sikhs is often made of wool and has one hundred and eight knots. Smaller malas of twenty-nine knots are also used.

There is a certain amount of ambivalence among Sikhs regarding the use of malas. Sometimes the material used in the beads is associated with a particular deity (e.g. tulsi beads are sacred to Vishnu), hence the Sikh preference for wool perhaps, and often malas are reputed to have protective powers, an idea which Sikhism does not accept, so many Sikhs would assert, with Guru Amar Das, 'Right deeds are the only effective mala, tell its beads with sincerity, for it keeps your soul company eternally' (AG 1134). It is also called a simarani.

Mālwā That part of Punjab south of the river Sutlej lying roughly between Ferozepore and Patiala.

Man A term difficult to render into English. It is a form of the word 'manas' which, in the *Rig Veda* means 'soul'. The usual translation 'mind' is scarcely adequate, for 'man' has to do with the whole area of inner thought and feeling. Meditation, the apprehension of truth, the experiences of love and grief, are among its functions. In a person who has not been liberated spiritually, the man is unreliable and has the potential for evil. 'The man is unsteady, it does not know the way. One who puts trust in his own man is as one befouled; he does not recognize the shabad' (AG 415).

On the other hand Guru Nanak can also say, 'The man is a priceless pearl. Dwelling on the name of God it has been accorded honour' (AG 22).

The evil influence of the man results in bondage to passion and especially self-centredness/self-reliance, **haumai**. The remedy lies in meeting the Guru and all that is implied by that phrase, becoming liberated through hearing and obeying the divine word.

Manī Siṅgh Bhāī (1644 – 1734) A devoted follower of the last four Gurus. Through his closeness to the ninth and tenth, (Guru Gobind Singh made him his steward, dewan, in 1691), he came to have an intimate knowledge of the Sikh movement. He was renowned as a preacher and interpreter of the scriptures (kathakar). After Guru Gobind Singh's death he was made administrator of the Darbar Sahib, a post which he held until his martyrdom. Just before he died he completed the compilation of the compositions of the Tenth Guru, the **Dasam Granth**. It is also said that he wrote a **janam sakhi** to which Guru Gobind Singh gave his approval. Unfortunately this seems no longer to exist; the one which bears his name is of a much later date.

Mañjī A word with two meanings when used in a Sikh context. The first, and present-day one, is the name given to the seat on which the Guru Granth Sahib is placed, respectfully known as the manji sahib. This is usually a stool or string-bed rather like a small charpoy; in fact, the word 'manji' is the Punjabi word for charpoy. It is also called a singhasan.

The significance of a manji lies in its use as the seat of a person in authority, other people sitting on the ground. This leads to its second meaning. To meet the needs of a geographically expanding Panth, Guru Amar Das divided it into twenty-two groups or manjis each under a sangatia responsible to himself. Their main duties were to preach, make decisions on minor matters concerning the affairs of the community, convey instructions from the Guru, and collect the daswandh (tithe). From the time of Guru Arjan the sangatias came to be known as **masands**, from a Persian word 'masnad', a synonym of manji.

During the later part of the seventeenth century the office of masand grew in importance; it often became hereditary, and its holders enjoyed a considerable degree of independence. A feature of Guru Gobind's policy was their abolition and the creation of the Khalsa, a body owing exclusive allegiance to himself, and developing the democratic ideal of the Guru Panth.

Man Mukh One whose man is dominated by haumai and who is therefore devoted to self-interest and evil. A fine description is given by Guru Nanak, which reads: 'Day and night are the two

103

seasons when he crops his land; lust and anger are his two fields. He waters them with greed, sows in them the seed of untruth, and his ploughman, wordly impulse, cultivates them. Evil thoughts are his plough, and evil the crop he reaps, for in accordance with the Divine Order, he cuts and eats' (AG 955). For the man mukh there is no hope, only death and rebirth.

Mantra See **Mūl Mantra**.

Mardānā (1459 – 1634) The close and lifelong companion of Guru Nanak, who was born in the same village, Talwandi. He was a Muslim of the low-caste group known as 'dum', whose traditional occupation was that of singing and dancing at festivals and weddings, activities which were regarded as despicable. Mardana was a skilled rebeck player who provided music to accompany the revelation which the Guru received. Three of his own compositions are included in the Guru Granth Sahib, on page 553.

Marriage See **Anaṇḍ Karāj** and **Lāvān**.

Martyr Persecution features prominently in the history of Sikhism. It annals are filled with stories of men, women and children who have given their lives rather than surrender their faith. These are known as shaheeds in the Sikh community and pictures of their sufferings are often to be seen in gurdwaras, beginning with the proto-martyr, Guru Arjan, who died in 1606. Some earlier words of his father are often called to mind and applied to such people: 'I anoint my countenace with dust from the feet of those who lovingly dedicate their bodies to God. They attain glory both here and hereafter' (AG 698).

Masaṅd Regional administrators first appointed by Guru Amar Das to oversee everyday organization of the Panth and the collection of financial contributions. Their influence grew, threatening the authority of the Gurus themselves, and they were abolished by **Guru Gobind Singh**. (See also **mañjī**.)

Masayā This term refers to the moonless night of the month. It is an even more popular occasion than usual for Sikhs to bathe in the waters of the sarovar at the Darbar Sahib in Amritsar. The practice is also followed at Taran Taran and many people will visit both places, walking in procession from the Akal Takht in Amritsar. This begins about ten o'clock at night; Taran Taran is reached in the early hours of the morning. On the way the pilgrims sing hymns. The tradition is traced back to the time of the Gurus; the procession by a group of Sikhs, known as chaunki, originated with Guru Arjan. A mela (fair) is held at Taran Taran. Mayasa is observed in some other parts of the Punjab, for example at Kartarpur in district Jullunder, and occasionally elsewhere. (See also **Puran Māshī**.)

Mata Sāhib Kaur Third wife of Guru Gobind Singh. Their marriage is described as kuwara dola, virgin wedlock, as it was not consumated. However, she was given the honour of being mother of the **Khalsa**, a status which is acknowledged and remembered at every initiation ceremony. The symbolic import- ance of her motherhood is considerable as it asserts that the Khalsa relationship is one which should transcend caste and family and social ties. For a woman to participate in the ritual preparation of **amrit** was probably a means of visibly rejecting notions of the polluting influence of women.

Mattā ṭekṇa The action of showing respect to the Guru Granth Sahib by touching the floor with one's forehead (matta), or placing the palms of the hands together in front of the forehead.

Māyā 'In the third watch of the night you fix your attention on wealth and the bloom of youthful beauty, you do not remember that Name of God which brings release. Forgetting God's Name, the soul is led astray through keeping maya's company. Absorbed in wealth, intoxicated by bodily beauty, it fritters its opportunity away' (AG 75).

These words describe a person who is suffering from the delusion of thinking that those things which are impermanent are goals worth pursuing. (The third watch which Guru Nanak mentions here is adulthood, the two coming before it being birth and childhood.)

Maya, in Sikh thought, is better translated as delusion, rather than illusion. The world, and the qualities described in the above quotation, are not unreal, they are ephemeral. Whoever becomes attached to maya, however, is doomed to rebirth, for maya is the antithesis of Truth. It 'makes us forsake the Lord' (AG 921). The antidote to maya is remembrance of God's Name, and the service of God in the company of like-minded people.

Guru Amar Das traced the progress of those who become ensnared by maya thus: 'A child is born when it pleases God, and the family rejoices. Love of the Lord departs, the child becomes attached to greed, and maya's writ begins to run. Such is maya, through which the Lord is forgotten. Worldly love wells up and one becomes attached to another. Says Nanak, those who enshrine love for the Lord, by God's grace obtain the Lord in the midst of maya' (AG 921).

Mazhabī Members of the sweeper, Chuhra, subcaste of what are now known as the scheduled classes, who have become Sikh. A group of chuhras recovered the head of Guru Tegh Bahadur after his execution in Delhi and conveyed it to his son who personally initiated them into the Panth, and gave them the title mazhabi, The Faithful Ones. Some of them served in the army and were given land settlements on discharge so that it is possible to come across Mazhabi villages rather than find members of the group scattered among other castes and discriminated against. Occasionally they are referred to as Ranghretas after the name of one of those who brought the ninth Guru's head to Guru Gobind Singh.

Melā The word may be used to refer to any fair, but in Sikhism it is related especially to such gatherings as the celebration of Baisakhi in Amritsar, or Hola Mohalla at Anandpur. It is used to denote any Sikh festival other than a gurpurb, the celebration of

106

the birth or death of a guru, and the anniversary of the installation of the Adi Granth at the Darbar Sahib in 1604.

Mīān Mīr (1550 – 1635) A Qadirite Sufi highly respected by Sikhs. He was a close spiritual companion of the fifth Guru as well as being influential at the Mughal court. He was present at the laying of the foundation stone of the Harmandir Sahib in 1589 and it is sometimes stated that he actually performed the ceremony at the invitation of Guru Arjan. However, the earliest accounts say that it was laid by the Guru himself. When the sixth Guru was imprisoned by the emperor Jehangir, Hazrat Mian Mir helped to obtain his release.

Milani The 'meeting' of the families which are to be united by marriage. That between male members is usually a public event taking place outside the bride's home or wherever the wedding is to be solemnized; the women will meet in private. Turban lengths or clothing are the usual gifts which are exchanged by those of equal rank in the two families, perhaps to the tenth or twelfth person and even beyond. The purpose of the ritual is to demonstrate the family hierarchies and to create a bond between them.

Mīṇās Literally, 'dissembling scoundrels', the term is the name given to those who followed Prithi Chand, brother of Arjan, and recognized him as Guru. It is claimed that they produced spurious hymns attributed to Guru Nanak in support of their case and that this was one of the reasons why Guru Arjan compiled the Adi Granth. The Minas no longer exist and knowledge of them is derived mainly from the writings of their opponents, but the memory of them is kept alive through the vow which Sikhs take during the amrit ceremony. They are one of five groups whose company the initiate must promise to spurn. The *Miharban Janam Sakhi* was also produced by Minas which means that some scholars have tended to regard it as an unreliable source.

Miracles At a popular level many Sikhs believe in miracles, and they abound in some of the janam sakhis. However, they were dismissed by the Gurus along with charms and incantations, partly because there were so many people who played upon susceptibilities of villagers to deprive them of the little wealth they had, but mainly because the Gurus rejected the idea of divine intervention to remedy, in some way, situations for which an omnipotent God must somehow be ultimately responsible. According to Bhai Gurdas, Guru Nanak told the Nath Yogis, who were famous for their occult powers, 'I have no miracle to display except the miracle of the True Name' (Var 1,verse 43).

Mīrī and Pīrī The two-sword doctrine of temporal (miri), and spiritual (piri) power. Certainly from the time of the sixth Guru, Sikhism became more than a spiritual path. The Gurus were men involved in political affairs as well as religious. Indeed as early as the time of Ram Das one of their titles had been Sacha Padsha, the True Sovereign, which was used by the Mughal emperors. Through miri and piri Sikhism asserts that there is really no such thing as a sacred-secular distinction. Sikhs are called to be saints and soldiers.

Misl A fighting unit in the Sikh armies of the eighteenth century. However, this definition should not necessarily convey the impression of unity of command or purpose. Sometimes there was intense rivalry between the commanders (misaldars), to whom soldiers might give greater loyalty than to the Panth. Nevertheless the heroism of the misls and their leaders has become legendary. (see also **Dal Khalsa**.)

Modern movements Since the early nineteenth century when physical threats to the existence of the community ceased, movements have existed which were committed to its spiritual reformation, especially the removal of Hindu influences which Sikhism had never shaken off at a popular level. The earliest were associated with such individuals as Dayal Das and Baba Ram Singh and resulted in the **Nirankari** and **Namdhari** movements.

Later, and partly to counter the missionary threats of Christianity and the Hindu **Arya Samaj**, the **Singh Sabha** movement developed as a response by the Panth as a whole. It was recognized that the education of Sikhs and the reform of religious practices could have only limited success if gurdwaras remained under the control of non-Sikhs and so the **Akali** movement came into being. Most of these movements still exist, but often in an institutionalized form not always obviously concerned with the issues which caused them to come into existence. (See also **Akālī Dal** and **Shromani Gurdwara Parbandhak Committee**).

Morchā Battlefront is the literal meaning of this word, which immediately conjures up an image of confrontation. Whenever Sikhs are convinced that the government is acting against their interests they are likely to declare a morcha and launch a protest in the form of mass agitation. This may include a bandh, the closing of shops and striking from work.

Mughal Empire Babur established his rule in Delhi in 1526 after invading India a few years earlier. From then until 1857 most of the country was under the nominal rule of the Mughal empire, though the southernmost part of India was never annexed and control began to pass to Indian rulers and the new invaders from Afghanistan and Europe during the eighteenth century.

Relationships between the Sikhs and the Mughals varied. Some compositions by Guru Nanak, the **Babur bani**, show him to have been deeply concerned by the invasion, though in it he saw the judgement of God. The **janam sakhis** speak of an encounter between the Guru and the Emperor at which a request for the release of non-combatant prisoners was made.

Each of the Gurus seems to have met one of the emperors or aroused political concern but of greatest importance in the earlier years of both the empire and the panth was the relationship with Akbar. This was good and the Sikhs prospered under his benign rule. However, with his death things changed dramatically. In

109

little more than a year the fifth Guru, who had been honoured by Akbar, was executed by his successor. Guru Hargobind seems to have enjoyed an ambiguous relationship with Jehangir, the ruler responsible for his father's death. At one time he was his prisoner, at others they hunted together. Shah Jehan, and after him Aurangzeb, pursued policies of Islamization which helped to provoke revolts in parts of the empire. The ninth and tenth Gurus may have been implicated in these though, on his death, Guru Gobind Singh was campaigning alongside the emperor Bahadur Shah in the Deccan.

The eighteenth century is seen by the Sikhs as a constant struggle for survival against Afghans and Mughals during which the **Dal Khalsa** was formed and an independent state of the Punjab was finally established. In the nineteenth century the threat from these two enemies was replaced by that of the British which culminated in the conquest of the Punjab in 1849.

Mukti Spiritual liberation is release from the round of death and rebirth to attainment of union with God. This state of bliss, which may be experienced in one's present human existence (see **jivaṇ mukti**), is beyond description but Guru Gobind Singh used the analogy of sparks rising from a fire and falling back into it, or drops of water returning to the stream. Guru Nanak spoke of singing God's praises in the divine presence, in God's court (diwan). As always, in the teachings of Guru Nanak, it is not discussion about such secondary matters that is important, but awareness of one's plight before liberation, knowledge of how to gain release, and encouragement to do something before it is too late. All this is summed up in a passage which rejects the merit of acquiring techniques of some aspects of Hinduism and asserts that only devotion to the divine Name has any worth. 'Sacrifices, burnt offerings, charity given to acquire merit, austerities, even worship, are all worthless, and the body continues to endure suffering. Without the Name of God there is no release. He who meditates on the Name, with the Guru's help, finds liberation. Without the Name birth into the world is fruitless. Without the

Name one eats poison, speaks evil, dies meritless, and so transmigrates' (AG 1127).

There are a number of places in the scriptures where devotion to God is seen as preferable to the desire for liberation, for example, 'Everyone longs for paradise, liberation, and heaven, and rests all hope on them. Those who desire a vision of God do not seek release, they are comforted and satisfied by that sight alone' (AG 1324). 'I desire neither worldly power nor liberation, . . . I desire nothing but seeing the Lord' (AG 534).

Whether the Guru is concerned that the desire for liberation can be selfish and result also in spiritual pride, or whether he wishes to stress the importance of devotion here and now as opposed to an emphasis on a future hope is not clear.

Mūl Mantra This is traditionally regarded as Guru Nanak's first poetical statement. It is a typically terse composition which almost defies translation. It may be paraphrased as follows:

This Being is One; the Truth; immanent in all things; sustainer of all things; creator of all things. Immanent in creation.

Without fear and without enmity. Not subject to time. Beyond birth and death. Self-manifesting. Known by the Guru's grace.

This is regarded as the essence of Sikh theology and its importance is underlined by giving it pride of place in the Guru Granth Sahib even before the **Japji**, Guru Nanak's most important shabad. In an abbreviated form it also stands at the head of each section or Rag.

The Mul Mantra is not esoteric. Unlike the mantras given by Hindu gurus to their chelas it may be disclosed to anyone though it is formally taught to candidates at the initiation ceremony.

Mundāvaṇī The literal meaning of this term is probably 'seal' rather than 'riddle' as suggested by some scholars, as it refers to a brief passage at the end of the Adi Granth intended to indicate that nothing else should be added. The verse of Guru Arjan's

111

describes the spiritual jewels contained in it: 'In the platter are placed three things, truth, contentment, and wisdom, as well as the nectar of the Lord's Name, the support of all.'

Nāgāra From the time of Guru Hargobind it has been customary for a kettledrum to be found in gurdwaras. He ordered it to be beaten when langar had been prepared. The drum symbolized freedom and was now combined with that which stood for the principle of equality and readiness to share one's wealth with others. It replaced the conch shell which had been used hitherto.

The nagara was used by rajas to welcome guests and as a symbol of authority. It is recorded that a Hindu prince, Raja Bhim Chand, in whose territory Anandpur was situated, challenged the right of the tenth Guru to use one, wishing to treat him as his subject.

Nāgar Kīrtan The literal meaning is 'town and songs of praise'. The phrase is used to describe the street processions which are a characteristic part of Indian religious celebrations. On the eve of a gurpurb or on the actual day, in the afternoon when the assembly gathered to hear speeches and kirtan has concluded with langar, the Guru Granth Sahib will be put on a decorated float together with singers (ragis), and poets, and taken through the streets. **Panj piare** carrying flags (nishan sahibs), will usually be at the head, followed by bands, perhaps children in school uniforms, and then the vehicle carrying the scripture, with more people walking behind it. The route to be taken may be decorated with arches and bunting.

Jalous is sometimes used as an alternative, but it can be applied to any kind of procession; nagar kirtan is more specific.

Nām This Punjabi word meaning 'Name' stands for 'the Name of God' and as such is one of the key words of Sikh theology. Nam is God manifest. Thus Guru Nanak could say, 'The self-existent God became manifest in Nam. Second came the creation of the universe' (AG 463).

Nam is all pervading, 'there is no place where Nam is not', he says (AG 4). Various names are used of God in the bani of Guru Nanak, such as Allah, Jagdish, Khuda or Gopal, but clearly Nam is something different, it is the expression of all that God is. Unlike these other names it had no immediate sectarian connotations, its meaning only became clear through experience, which, for the Gurus, was the only way that God could be known. It was their task to make people aware of this truth so that they might be filled with Nam.

'Nam, the immaculate is unfathomable. How can it be known? Nam is within us, how can it be reached? It is Nam that works everywhere and permeates all space. The perfect Guru awakens your heart to the vision of Nam. It is by God's grace that one comes to such enlightenment' (Guru Ram Das AG 1242).

Frequently Sat Nam, the True Name, is used by the Gurus rather than Nam alone. Like Nam, Truth is not an abstract proposition, it is known experientially. Hence the emphasis in Sikh teaching upon meditation on Nam, **Nam Simran**, and truthful living.

Nāmdev A tailor or calico printer from Maharasthra, usually included in list of the sants of north India. The year 1270 is given as that of his birth but his length of life is uncertain. He is one of the bhagats whose compositions, sixty in number, were included in the Adi Granth. In the sections where they are to be found they come third in order, after those of Kabir and Sheikh Farid.

Nāmdhāri A Sikh movement which originated in the nineteenth century and played an important part in the Indian freedom struggle. It began with Baba Balak Singh (1799 – 1861), and developed under the leadership of his successor Baba Ram Singh. He came from Bhaini Sahib near Ludhiana, which is now the main centre of the movement. Initially Namdhari protest was against moral laxity within the Panth, especially the use of drugs, alcohol, meat eating, and personal extravagence particularly in the form of marriage rituals and dowries. Intercaste marriage and the remarriage of widows were also advocated. In 1872 Baba Ram Singh was deported by the British to Rangoon for causing disturbances, and sixty-six of his followers were executed by being tied to the mouths of canons which were then fired. They had attacked Muslim slaughterhouses and butchers' shops as part of a campaign to restore Sikh rule to the Punjab.

It is basic to namdhari teachings that Guru Gobind Singh did not die in 1708 but survived until 1812 having conferred guruship on Baba Balak Singh. Namdharis also believe that Satguru Ram Singh is still alive and will return from Burma to lead them. Meanwhile his descendent, Satguru Jagjit Singh, provides the movement with guidance.

Namdharis may be recognized by the white turbans laid flat across the forehead. They observe the strict code of behaviour of Baba Balak Singh, and wedding ceremonies are performed around the fire (havan). They are sometimes called Kukas because of a cry often made at the singing of hymns. They commonly use a woollen mala of 108 knots in their devotions.

Names In the Indian tradition men and women usually have three names; first that which they are given, secondly one of the given names of a parent, and finally, the family name from which a person's caste, varna, or subgroup, jati ('zat' in Punjabi), and gotra (Punjabi 'got'), can be adduced. Sikhism's naming system may be seen as a reaction against this tradition.

The emphasis is placed upon the middle name, Kaur meaning princess in the case of woman, and Singh, lion, for men. These were given to all Sikhs when the Khalsa was instituted at Baisakhi in 1699. By adopting them Sikhs demonstrated that they were all sons and daughters of the same parents, the Guru and his wife, and that this kinship replaced that based on varna, jati or gotra. This has not happened in its entirety; the old names are sometimes still used for a variety of reasons, one being a practical one, as anyone trying to find the right Singh in a London telephone directory knows. The first name is given by the family after consulting the Guru Granth Sahib. One point may be made

114

about these, many of them can be common to males and females, for example, Amarjit, Jaswant, or Avtar.

Nâm japṇâ, kīrt karṇâ, vand chakṇâ Meditation on God's name, honest work, and giving to those in need. These are the three major characteristics of Sikh spirituality and morality. In early teaching the discipline or **dharma** was often said to consist of 'nam, dan, ishnan', keeping the Divine Name always in mind, ordering one's life so as to be independent of others but always ready to give help; and purity of mind, body, clothing, house, and conduct. In essence the two expressions are the same.

Nâm Simraṇ The literal meaning of this phrase is 'God remembrance', and it is often translated as prayer or meditation. Perhaps 'to hold God constantly in mind' is more accurate, though wordy, for although the Gurus prescribed certain times for practising Nam Simran they taught that nothing less than being filled with Nam should be the goal of life. Guru Nanak described it as the antidote to the poison of pain, which permeates the whole body in the same way, but with wholesome consequences. These quotations from Guru Nanak give some idea of the purpose and consequences of Nam Simran and may guard against the view that it is a formal exercise.

'One who is steeped in Nam is freed from haumai, is gathered up in the True One, meditates on the way of true yoga, finds the door of salvation, acquires understanding of the three worlds, and attains eternal peace' (AG 941; the Guru was addressing Nath Yogis).

'If the mind is defiled by impurity it is cleansed with love of Nam. Virtue and impurity are not mere words; we carry the influence of what we have done with us. As you have sown so shall you reap, and in accordance with the divine order (hukam) you will transmigrate' (AG 4).

Another phrase used synonymously with nam simran is nam japna, repetition of God's Name: 'If I repeat the Name I live; if I forget it I die. Repeating the Name of the True One is hard, but if one hungers for it and partakes of it all sadness goes' (AG 9 and 349).

Nam Simran is primarily an individual act of meditation but is sometimes undertaken by groups. A **mala** may be used but this is not essential. Though early morning and evening are the times of day commended by the Gurus, the aim, the attainment of mystical union with God, not the method, is what should concern the Sikh.

Nānak, Gurū (15 April 1469 – 22 September 1539) The first Guru was born into a Hindu family in the Muslim-owned village of Talwandi which now lies in that part of Punjab which is in Pakistan. He was a **khatri** by birth, regarded by Sikhs to be part of the kshatria varna of Hinduism, and of the Bedi subgroup. He was employed as a storekeeper-accountant to a Muslim govenor of the town of Sultanpur, Daulat Khan Lodi.

Sikhs believe that the Guru's birth was non-karmic, that is that he was born in response to God's will as someone already in a state of enlightenment. He was to be God's messenger to the kal yug, the present age in which God, righteousness and justice had been forgotten. This may provide the key to understanding the words which he spoke at the very beginning of his ministry.

When he was about thirty years old Nanak went missing after taking his customary morning bath in the nearby river. Three days later he returned to his friends and pronounced 'There is no Hindu, there is no Muslim, so whose path shall I follow? God is neither Hindu nor Muslim, and the path I shall follow is God's.' This, he said, he had learned during his absence when he had been taken to God's court and commissioned to be his messenger. (The experience is described in AG 150.) It would seem that the Guru, believing that the two existing paths had lost sight of spirituality in concentrating on rituals, felt called to offer a message through which liberation, not attachment, could be achieved. Leaving home and family, he spent the next thirty years travelling widely preaching his message in the form of poetical compositions, bhajans, to which his companion, the Muslim **Mardana**, provided a musical accompaniment.

Although Guru Nanak undoubtedly wished for religious harmony, the purpose of his mission was not to unite Hindu and Muslim as has often been suggested. Still less was it a wish to create a new religion. Rather it was to assure men and women that spiritual liberation was available to everyone and help them to realize it.

Guru Nanak settled at Kartarpur, a village on the river Ravi when he was over fifty years old, probably in 1521, and there established what is regarded as the ideal Sikh community. Although he did not regard himself as a Guru in the traditional Hindu sense, always asserting that God was the Guru and Nanak only a 'lowly bard' (AG 150), he nevertheless found it necessary to provide a successor to care for the men and women who had come to depend on him for spiritual guidance.

Portraits of Guru Nanak date from the eighteenth century and depict him as keeping two pre-**Khalsa** aspects of the Sikh form, the turban and uncut hair, represented by the beard. His clothing resembles neither that of Hindu nor Muslim holy men but something of both, as described in the **janam sakhis**. Pictorial representations of the Gurus are to be found in most homes and many gurdwaras, but Sikhs should not bow towards them and they not be placed in such a position that they might seem to rival the unique status of the **Guru Granth Sahib**. Guru Nanak and his successors are to be respected as men through whom the word of God was revealed, but they were only human beings, the word lives on in the scripture and community.

Nānak panthi A follower of Guru Nanak. The phrase is sometimes used to make a distinction between emphasis upon devotionalism and the formalism which is perceived to be the way in which the **Khalsa** ideal has developed. Khalsa Sikhs would regard this as a false antithesis and express their concern with a

117

life-style which may give little attention to keeping the turban and **five Ks**, and other aspects of the **Rahit Maryada**.

Nānaksar Nanaksar is a site near Kaleran, a village in the Punjab where a Sikh called Baba Nand Singh used to meditate. It lies about forty-five kilometres west of Ludhiana. A beautiful gurdwara now stands on the site and provides a pilgrimage centre for devotees attracted by his teaching and personality. Besides the emphasis on spirituality associated with all such *sant*-inspired movements, there are certain distinctive features. Some members adopt a celibate life and dress uniformly in white. These are called 'bahingams'. Vegetarianism is encouraged. Each full moon (puranmashi), there is an all-night celebration of the birth of Guru Nanak. The Guru Granth Sahib is given particular respect. In a gurdwara this may be seen in the practice of having a number of copies installed rather than one as is found elsewhere. Portraits of Guru Nanak show him sitting in the traditional posture of meditation with a lotus mark (padam), on one foot. Accommodation is set aside for Bhai Mani Singh who succeeded Baba Nand Singh who died in his seventies round about 1943. Nanaksar gurdwaras are to be found in Britain, North America and Africa, as well as India, though the number of devotees is not large.

Nanded The town in the Deccan where Guru Gobind Singh died. It is now one of the five **takhts** of the Sikh religion.

Nandlāl, Bhāī (1633 – 1713) A poet, well versed in Arabic and Persian. He was born in Agra and spent much of his life as an administrator in Mughal service. He became influenced by Sikh teachings and from about 1697 was a close companion of the tenth Guru. His ten books in praise of the Gurus and on the subject of Sikh philosophy are accorded the honour and distinction, along with the works of Bhai Gur Das, of being read and used as commentaries in gurdwaras, though they do not enjoy the status of the Guru Granth Sahib and *Dasam Granth*. The *Rahit Nama* and *Tankhanama* are Bhai Nandlal's best known writings.

Nankānā Sāhib The modern name of the village where Guru Nanak was born, then known as Talwandi. It is now in Pakistan, Sikhs frequently make pilgrimages to it and some would like it to be given the status of an internationally respected holy city outside the jurisdiction of a particular government.

Nāth Tradition See **Haṭha Yoga**.

Nāth Yoga The name is given to the teachings and practices of a number of groups which are united in a common allegiance to **Gorakhnath**, the use of the techniques of **hatha yoga**, and the custom of wearing large ear-rings known as mudras, from which they get the name Kanphat yogis (split-eared) by which they are sometimes known. Their origins lie in esoteric tantrism, the use of practices based on texts containing dialogues between Shiva and his consort Parvati, representing energy or power. The purpose, to obtain liberation, was sometimes accompanied by one of acquiring power over others, in the view of the Sikh Gurus. Clearly Guru Nanak knew the naths well and took them very seriously. He makes use of their terminology but has little time for their way of life which he considered to be parasitic. They withdrew from the world but depended for life upon the generosity of villagers to whom they came with their begging bowls, and who may have lived in fear of their supposed supernatural powers.

Perhaps the following passage sums up his view as well as any: 'A man may plait his hair into a crown, cover his body with ashes and discard his clothes altogether. Without God's name he will not find satisfaction. He assumes the dress of his order but is bound to the deeds of his previous life' (AG 1127).

Nihang 'Crocodile' or 'carefree' may be found as translations of this term depending on how its etymology is traced. The first interpretation can be linked with their battle formation, the second with their detachment from all things which might hinder their total devotion to the Sikh cause, as well as to their complete disregard of personal safety in serving it.

Nihangs were men who could be relied upon to defend desperate situations to the death in the army of Guru Gobind Singh. Their prominence increased in the eighteenth century when, as cavalry units, they harrassed the Mughal and Afghan forces which were operating in the Punjab. In the nineteenth century they were often known as **Akalis** and took part in the struggle for control of those gurdwaras which were in the hands of Hindu **mahants**.

Nihangs are easily recognizable from the uniform of blue robe with a yellow sash, and large blue turban, often with two or three quoits of steel fastened round it. The weapons they carry may be old fashioned or modern. Nihangs usually live in groups in encampments outside towns. Traditionally they reject the comfort of houses or tents, using only the blankets they carry in their backpacks.

Nirankār Sikhism teaches that God is 'the eternally unchanging Formless One' (AG 3), Nirankar. This not only means that God must be understood as pure spirit, to whom the epithets of male or female cannot be appropriately applied, it also carries with it the rejection of the belief that God assumes form, be it human or animal. This, on the one hand, denies the Hindu doctrine of avatar, it also warns against any attempts to assert that the Sikh Gurus were more than human. However, Guru Nanak could speak of blending with the Formless One, and consequently he is sometimes described as 'Nanak Nirankari': 'Formless One, beyond fear and enmity, I blend in your pure light' (AG 596).

Nirankāri An important nineteenth century Sikh reform movement founded by Dayal Das who died in 1855. At a time when Hindu influences were strong and statues of deities were to be found in many gurdwaras, he inspired an emphasis upon the Guru Granth Sahib and based naming, marriage, and death rituals upon it. The character of Sikh ceremonies today owes much to this movement.

Nirankaris prefer this name to Sikh because of the description of the first Guru as Nanak Nirankari, and place the emphasis upon spirituality rather than what they regard as the militant ideals of the Khalsa. For a variety of reasons the Nirankaris have become what might be called a sect, using the term in a sociological sense, on the fringe of Sikhism. They have a Guru, Gurdev Singh, and this and their general distinctiveness, has caused tension within the Panth. The headquarters of the movement is at Chandigarh.

Nirguṇa Without qualities, or perhaps, more accurately beyond qualities, in a theological sense, for Sikh teaching is that God 'has neither form nor material attributes' (AG 750), but has 'a thousand eyes, yet not one' (AG 663). Being devoid of qualities God is beyond human knowledge and comprehension, but God became saguna, 'with attributes', for the purpose of revelation, both in creation and, especially as **Guru**. In the Hindu **bhakti** tradition God becomes saguna by adopting a physical form and descending into the world. This doctrine of **avatar** is totally rejected by the Sikh Gurus, Guru Nanak expressed the Sikh doctrine thus: 'From the absolute condition, the Pure One became manifest, from nirguna becoming saguna' (AG 940 line 14).

Nirmalās An ascetic order of Sikhs, from the word 'nirmal' meaning 'without blemish'. They wear ochre robes like Hindu ascetics and observe their birth and death rituals. Their centre, called an akhara (literally 'wrestling ground'), is at Hardwar. The group originates from five men who were sent by Guru Gobind Singh to study at the great Hindu centre of learning, Varanasi. They then set up schools for the instruction of Sikhs, but had themselves become affected by their own contacts with Hindu thought. They also served as missionaries and during the eighteenth century were often mahants or gurdwaras. It is said that Nirmalas were the first Sikhs to use the Khanda as the Sikh emblem or symbol.

121

Nishān Sāhib (niśān sāhib) A gurdwara may easily be recognized by the flag which waves over it. This is the Nishan Sahib. 'Nishan' simply means 'flag'; the word 'sahib' is frequently attached to places or artefacts as a mark of respect. The flag should be yellow in colour, is usually triangular in shape, and bears the Khanda symbol on it. Sometimes this is also to be seen at the head of the flag pole.

The use of the Nishan Sahib originated with Guru Hargobind. Before his time there was nothing to indicate a Sikh building. The use of the **Khanda** is much later, probably nineteenth century. It may have been added by **Nirmala** Sikhs. Five Nishan Sahibs are often carried in front of the Guru Granth Sahib in Sikh street processions, known as **nagar kirtan**, on occasions such as gurpurbs.

Nishkam Sēwak Jathā A reform movement which originated in Britain inspired by Sant Puran Singh (died 1983). He lived in Kenya, at Kericho, for many years, and is often called Kerichowale Baba. He encouraged Sikhs to take **amrit** and observe the tenents of the faith fully, especially the prohibition of alcohol, and the practice of **nam simran**. Its members are vegetarian and place considerable emphasis upon **akhand paths**, continuous readings of the complete Guru Granth Sahib.

Nitnem Personal devotion is something which each of the Gurus practised and required of their followers. This has become formalized in the Daily Rule, for which the Punjabi term is 'Nitnem'. This consists of reading or reciting, and meditating upon, the **Japji** of Guru Nanak, the Jap and Ten Swayyas of Guru Gobind Singh in the morning; at sunset Sodar **Rahiras**, a collection of nine hymns of the first, third and fifth Gurus; and, before going to bed, Kirtan **Sohila**, five hymns by the same three Gurus. It is usual for Sikhs to have a small book, known as a Nitnem, which contains these compositions and the Sikh prayer, **Ardas**, and for it to be treated with much of the respect accorded

122

the Guru Granth Sahib; for example, hands will be washed before using it, and it may be wrapped in cloth when it is not being read.

Oaṅkār(u) The title of one of Guru Nanak's lengthiest compositions which is found between pages 929 and 938 of the Adi Granth, and also the word which stands for God as Primal Being, as Omkara (Om), in Sanskrit, from which it is derived. In the hymn Oankar is described as the creator of Brahma and the Vedas, the most sacred of Hindu scriptures, as well as the one who made the universe. The inevitable fate of birth and rebirth, irrespective of wealth, class or intellect is stressed as usual in the Guru's teachings. The answer to the question, 'How can I be released?' is through God the Guru's mercy and grace and by meditating upon God in one's heart (with sincerity). 'Worldly affairs and wanderings come to an end when the Name's bliss enters the human mind' (AG 934 line 16).

Pacifism There has sometimes been a tendency to regard Guru Nanak as a pacifist and later Gurus as militants who changed the principles of Sikhism. This view is unacceptable on two counts. First, there is no evidence for the claim that Guru Nanak was a pacifist. He spoke against the brutality of the invading Mughal armies but had little opportunity to affect events by any actions of his own. The young community was insignificant in numbers and influence. Secondly, Guru Gobind Singh summed up the Sikh view of the use of force when he said, 'When all other means have failed it is justified to use the sword'. His own conduct may be said to illustrate the requirement for warfare to be restrained and disciplined. (See **dharam yudh**). Tradition recognizes that the sword (**kirpan**), is not merely a symbolic or ceremonial part of the dress of a Sikh, and implicitly acknowledges that Sikhs should respond to the call of religion or country to fight, but otherwise life should be lived under the legal restraints of the state. Among those Sikhs who keep the five Ks there must therefore be a readiness to engage in warfare. There are others, who would describe themselves as **Nanak pathis** or emphasize

sikhi, the spiritual ideals of Guru Nanak as they understand them, who might be pacifist. However, the numbers cannot be estimated and would only become clear if the country in which they were living had a system of conscription.

Pada A division of a hymn (shabad), in the Guru Granth Sahib. It may vary in length from one to four verses.

Pagri Punjabi word for 'Turban'. Sometimes 'pag' is also used.

Pālki The structure in which the Guru Granth Sahib is ceremonially installed, resembling a palanquin, a word to which palki is related.

Pallā The scarf, usually pink or red in colour, which a groom carries at the engagement and wedding ceremonies.

Pangat The literal meaning is that of all people sitting together in rows for community dining. It is therefore used to refer to the dining hall where people of all castes, classes, and religions may eat together. Often the term **langar**, which strictly speaking refers to the meal, is used instead of pangat.

Pāñj Kakke Punjabi name for the Five Ks which must be worn by Sikhs who have been initiated into the **Khalsa**. See **kachh, kanghā, kara, kes,** and **kirpān**.

Pāñj Piāre On 30 March by the calendar then in use, (13 April according to the Gregorian calendar), **Guru Gobind Singh** instituted the **Khalsa**. In response to his call for Sikhs to come forward who would be willing to lay down their lives, five men eventually offered themselves. These founding members of the Khalsa have passed into history as the Panj Piare. They were,
Bhai Daya Singh, a khatri of Lahore in Punjab;
Bhai Dharam Singh, a Jat of Rohtak in Punjab;
Bhai Mohkam Singh, a washerman (dhobi) of Dwarka in Gujarat;

Bhai Sahib Singh, a barber (nai) of Bidar in Maharashtra;
Bhai Himat Singh, a water carrier (jhiwar) of Puri in Orissa.
They are remembered in the prayer Ardas which is used in public
worship.

The expression is also used of the executive committees
appointed to look after the five **Takhts**, of the five people who
conduct the amrit sanskar (initiation ceremony), the five who
carry **nishan sahibs** before the Guru Granth Sahib in processions,
and of the five people of good standing which a family may ask to
eat with them on certain joyful occasions such as the birth of a
child. When **karah parshad** is distributed five small portions
may be rolled into balls and given to five respected members of
the sangat before the rest are served.

Panth This word of Sanskrit origin literally refers to a path or
way, but is now used to describe groups who follow a particular
teacher or doctrine. It is the name used by Sikhs to describe the
community. The word 'sangat' is given to a particular congregation gathered for worship or some similar activity.

Parbhat Pheries Parbhat means 'early morning', pheri means
'to go round'. The term is a name given to groups of devout
persons who go round the streets singing hymns to remind people
of a coming celebration.

Parchār/prachār 'Preaching'. Sometimes used of missionary
work but also of preaching intended to recall the lapsed or lax to
serious religious observance and keeping the Sikh discipline.

Parkarmā (parikarmā) The walkway around the pool for
bathing (sarovar) found at many gurdwaras. Sikhs will always go
along it in a clockwise direction, to receive God's grace in the
right hand, not the left which is considered unclean.

Parkash karṇā 'Making manifest'. The early morning ceremony, (at **amritvela**), when the Guru Granth Sahib is formally

125

opened and the day's worship begins. The nature of the rituals vary depending on where the scripture has been kept overnight. If it has only been covered by a cloth, **rumala**, the Sikh prayer, **Ardas**, will be said, the coverings removed, and the book will be opened at random and a reading taken (**vak**). If it has been placed in a bed or otherwise kept in a special room set aside for the purpose, Ardas will be said there and the Guru Granth Sahib will be carried on the head of a Sikh with others following in procession, and then placed on its throne (palki) in the gurdwara. The opening ceremony described above will then commence.

Parmānand A brahmin of Barsi near Pandhapur in the Bombay region. The dates of his birth and death are not known. One of his hymns is included in the Guru Granth Sahib, on page 1253.

Paṭh A reading from the Guru Granth Sahib. It is most commonly used to describe a complete non-stop reading, **akhand path**, lasting about forty-eight hours, or one which may take place over a longer period, a sidharan path, which is not continuous.

Patit A lapsed Sikh (literally 'fallen'), who has failed to observe the Code of Discipline. Strictly speaking it refers to those who have been initiated and failed to live up to their vows but it is used in a general way of anyone who has, for example, shaved the beard or cut the hair.

Patka A covering sometimes worn between the hair and the turban. It may also be used as a head-covering by boys or by sportsmen.

Paṭnā Sāhib The birthplace of Guru Gobind Singh in Bihar. It is now one of the five **takhts**.

Pauṛī 'Staircase', 'stanza', a common name given to verses in the Guru Granth Sahib. Its length and metre are both variable.

126

Peerha A woman appointed to minister to the needs of women members of the Sikh community and to act as a missionary to women. Guru Amar Das was the initiator of this practice. The plural form is 'peerhian' but sometimes 'peerhas' is found. A peerhi is a stool about thirty-five centimetres square with a seat made of string.

Pherā 'Circling' of the Guru Granth Sahib during the wedding ceremony. As this takes place during the reading of the wedding hymn known as **Lavan** the circlings, four times in a clockwise direction, are often called 'phere' (the plural form of the word).

Pilgrimage Although Sikhs may make a pilgrimage to the Darbar Sahib, the Golden Temple, at Amritsar, strictly speaking tiraths, place of pilgrimage, have no importance and belief in the efficacy of visiting them or bathing in the waters of sacred rivers is discouraged. Guru Amar Das said, 'The world is smeared with the dirt of egoism and duality. Impurity is not removed by washing at holy places' (AG 39).

Guru Nanak stated that the only way to achieve cleansing was through faith in God, the Satguru: 'There is no place of pilgrimage like the Guru who alone is the pool of compassion and contentment' (AG 687).

Despite this Guru Amar Das did provide Sikhs with a tirath, the bathing place or **baoli** at Goindwal. This was to wean them away from visiting Hardwar and is indicative of the powerful residual hold which Hindu practices and ideas had upon those who were joining the Panth.

Pipa A Rajput prince who was once a devotee of Durga but became a disciple of **Ramanand**, the great medieval guru, and is included in the list of his most important missionary followers. A single hymn composed by him is included in the Adi Granth, on page 695.

Pollution The important Hindu concepts of purity and pollution are rejected by Sikhism. Guru Nanak considered only moral cleanliness to have any worth and devotion to God as the sole method of achieving it. He said, 'If the mind is unclean, it cannot be purified by worshipping stones, visiting holy places, and wandering about like an ascetic. Only one who cherishes the True Lord acquires honour' (AG 586).

Pothī A book or volume, frequently used of a collection of hymns in Sikh writings. The janam sakhis refer to one carried by Guru Nanak on his visit to Mecca. Guru Arjan used the Mohan Pothi, compiled by Guru Amar Das but in the ownership of his son Mohan, when compiling the Adi Granth.

Prayer The Sikh emphasis is upon **nam simran**, God-mindfulness, achieved through meditation, but at all ceremonies the formal prayer **Ardas** is offered and a Sikh should use it daily in personal devotions. Petitionary prayer has its place in Sikhism. Guru Nanak said, 'Whoever cries out and begs at God's door will be heard and blessed' (AG 349). **Kirtan**, meaning singing God's praises, is the form which corporate worship takes and serves as a reminder, together with the popular name for God, Wahiguru, Wonderful Lord, that prayer may include adoration.

Priest Guru Nanak reacted strongly against the belief that a particular class of people were divinely appointed by birth or some ritual to perform religious acts on behalf of others. He accused brahmins of exploitation and refused to believe in their authority or that of the *Vedas*. There is a tendency among Sikhs and media reporters to use the word 'priest' when referring to **jathedars** or **granthis**, but it should be avoided.

Prithī Chand Older brother of Guru Arjan. He felt that he should have been designated Guru by his father and opposed the leadership of his brother. In 1606 he tried to succeed him unsuccessfully. His followers were given the name 'Minas', dissemblers, from a robber tribe of that name, by the Panth. Although they are now extinct, they may have survived until the

128

end of the seventeenth century at least, as they are mentioned as one of the five groups which Guru Gobind Singh execrated, telling **Khalsa** members to have no dealings with them. The injunction is still included in the words of the initiation ceremony.

Puñjāb The name means 'land of the five rivers', which are the Sutlej, Beas, Ravi, Chenab, and Jhelum. It is regarded by Sikhs as their homeland for it is the region in which their religion began and where it has always been based. Apart from converts, Sikhs wherever they live are of Punjabi origin, their home language is usually Punjabi and this is also the language of worship. Geographically, the Punjab stretched from Afghanistan and Kashmir almost to Delhi in the days of Maharaja Ranjit Singh. Now the term tends to be used of the Indian state of the Punjab, in which Sikhs form a bare majority of the population, some fifty-two per cent. (The spelling Panjab is preferred by some writers.)

Puran Máshī Observances on the night of the full moon are against the strict teachings of Sikhism. However, according to the Bala janam sakhi, Guru Nanak was born on this night in the month Kartik, Samvat era 1526, and some sangats commemorate the occasion monthly or less frequently. On 20 October, the equivalent in the Gregorian calendar of Kartik puran mashi, is celebrated the Guru's birthday in keeping with a long-established tradition even though scholars now prefer the date of 15 April given in other janam sakhis.

Qaum A term becoming popular among some Sikh writers to describe the Panth. It can have the same meaning but may also be used as it is seen to have an additional implication of 'nation'. There is often concern among some Sikhs that they should be regarded as a nation not merely a religion. This is linked with demands for self-government or independence for the Punjab.

Rádhásoámí A movement which began in Agra in 1861 as a result of the teaching of Shiv Dayal Singh. Its main centre is now at Beas in the Punjab. Its teachings include belief in a living Guru, the present one is Charan Singh, the householder way of life, bodily care — through the rejection of drugs, alcohol, and meat — self-discipline through the practice of yoga, and tapping into the Sound Current, the vibrations of the Supreme Creator, also by yogic meditation. The background of its Guru has been Sikh and therefore it is sometimes regarded as a form of Sikhism. This it is not. Its focus is the teachings of its own Gurus, not the Guru Granth Sahib. Some individual Sikhs are Radhasoami devotees.

Rág A tune or the series of five or more notes upon which it is based. The term is derived from the word 'rang' meaning colour indicating that the music is intended to evoke certain feelings. Therefore, with the exception of the Japji all the hymns of the Adi Granth are set to specific rags so that spiritual development may result from a combination of word and sound. It must be remembered that Mardana was the constant companion of Guru Nanak, always available to add inspired music to the hymns (bani), which the Guru was inspired to compose.

Rágī A musiciian who leads and accompanies the singing of kirtan, the hymns of the Guru Granth Sahib in the gurdwara.

Rág Mālā The last poetical composition included in the Adi Granth. It is a catalogue of rags used in Indian music of the time (the beginning of the seventeenth century). Not all of the eighty-four listed are found in the Adi Granth.

Rahirās The sunset liturgy, sometimes also known as Sodar Rahiras, comprises nine hymns. Four of these are by Guru Nanak, three by Guru Ram Das, and the rest by Guru Arjan. They are to be found at the beginning of the Guru Granth Sahib immediately after the Japji, though each is also placed elsewhere in the scripture under the appropriate raga. There is also supplementary material, the **Chaupai** of Guru Gobind Singh, six verses of the Anand by Guru Amar Das, and the **Mundavani** and a concluding couplet by Guru Arjan.

Rahit Conduct or discipline. It may be applied generally to the codes of conduct laid down by the Gurus but now is often used as an abbreviated form of **Rahit Maryada**.

Rahit Maryādā The Sikh Code of Conduct accepted in 1945 was the result of many years of research and discussion. There was no disputing the fact that Guru Gobind Singh had provided the Khalsa with a disciplinary code when he instituted it, but its precise form was a matter for argument. Extant codes dating from the eighteenth century contained many embellishments and interpolations which clearly contradicted the principles of the Guru. Between 1931 and 1945 the **Shromani Gurdwara Parbandhak Committee** attempted to produce an acceptable Rahit. It was successful where other efforts had failed and the resulting Rahit Maryada was, approved by the S.G.P.C. on 3 February 1945. It is now the standard against which Sikh individuals and communities should measure themselves. That is not to say that it is followed in every particular but it has brought a considerable level of uniformity to the Panth.

Rahit Nāmā A manual of conduct laying down the rules by which a **Khalsa** Sikh's life should be ordered. It covers spiritual discipline as well as social relationships and ethics. A number of Rahit Namas survive from the eighteenth century, each purporting to be based on the injunctions of Guru Gobind Singh.

Rāj Karegā Khālsā 'The Khalsa shall rule'. This became the war cry and slogan of the Sikhs during the eighteenth century. The verse, in its entirety reads: 'The Khalsa shall rule, no hostile refractory shall exist. Frustrated they shall all submit, and those who come in for shelter shall be protected.' It was evidently composed and first used by the Khalsa in the time of Banda Singh Bahadur, political leader of the Sikhs from 1710 to his execution in 1716 in their resistance to the Emperor Bahadur Shah who had issued edicts for the execution of all 'disciples of Nanak'. The first line, 'Raj karega Khalsa yaqi rahe na koe' is said at the end

131

of the prayer, **Ardas**, at the end of congregational worship. It gives psychological uplift and is regarded as a prophetic promise.

Rāmānand The most famous of the Hindu teachers whose works are included in the **bhagat bani**, though he is represented by only one hymn, on page 1195 of the Adi Granth. Tradition states that he was the guru of Kabir, Ravidas (Rai Das), and many other medieval Indian saints, but this seems to be the result of attempts either to enhance his importance or to provide brahmin gurus for religious preceptors who had no right to exercise that function, not being brahmins themselves. Clearly their devotees could not conceal their caste or, more usually outcaste status, but they could claim that they were disciples of a brahmin, the next best thing. The year 1299 may have been that of his birth, but this has often been put later by those who accept that he was Kabir's guru (1440 – 1518 are dates often favoured for Kabir, consequently Ramanand is dated 1400 – 1470). The best that can be said is that the period of his life is uncertain, and the traditions linking him with the men mentioned above are unreliable and unlikely to be true. It is perhaps interesting to note that no attempt was made to link Ramanand and Guru Nanak; a reason could be the suggestion that Kabir provided the connection, but more likely it is explained by the adamant rejection by the Sikhs of any brahmin influence.

(The link with Kabir and the problem of dating are discussed in *Kabir*, C.Vaudeville, Oxford, 1974.)

Rām Dās, Gurū (born 24 September 1534, Guru September 1 1574 to September 1 1581). Son-in-law of the third Guru. Founder of the town now known as Amritsar which he made the focal point for Baisakhi and Diwali gatherings of the Panth. He also composed the wedding hymn, **Lavan**, used at Sikh marriage ceremonies. He established the line of Sodhi Gurus which lasted until 1708 when Guru Gobind Singh conferred guruship on the scripture. Six hundred and seventy-nine of his compositions are contained in the Adi Granth.

Rāmgaṛhīā Ramgarhias are Sikhs of the tarkhan, carpenter, caste in the main though they also include some members from the Lohar, blacksmith, Raj, masons and bricklayers castes, which now constitute a distinctive and exclusively Sikh jati. They take their name from Jassa Singh, a tarkhan who commanded one of the Sikh misls in the eighteenth century and is renowned for his government and defence of the Ramgarth fort in Amritsar. Ramgarhias are to be found in the towns rather than the countryside though many are now landowners. It was their artisan skills which brought them to the notice of the British who encouraged them to move to East Africa in the last decade of the nineteenth century to open up the country by building its transport infrastructure. With Africanization many descendants of these migrants moved to the United Kingdom and others went to North America. Ramgarhias are also keenly interested in education. Today they are to be found in all walks of life but especially in occupations associated with the new technology. The former president of India, Zail Singh, is a Ramgarhia.

Rām Rāi Son of Guru Har Rai. His father sent him to the Mughal court to answer charges that the Adi Granth contained material defamatory to Islam. He was required to explain some words by Guru Nanak, 'The dust of a Muslim is kneaded by a potter into clay, he converts it into pots and bricks which cry out as they burn' (AG 466).

He blamed a scribal error, saying that 'Mussulman' should have read 'beiman', faithless. On learning of this act of cowardice which also allowed the impression to be obtained that the scripture could be subject to human error, the Guru rejected his son forbidding him ever to enter his presence again. Ram Rai remained at the Mughal court where he became the focus of attempts to have him installed as Guru when his father died.

Rām Rāj The rule of Rama which is regarded as a golden act when righteousness flourished. Sikhs look forward to its restoration and sometimes express the view that it will come when the Khalsa rules. (See **Raj Karega Khalsa**.) In this way they indicate that its rule will not be sectarian but secular in the Indian sense of that term, that is the state will respect all religions without being partial to any. The term was made popular by Mahatma Gandhi.

Rañjīt Siṅgh, Mahārājā 1780 – 1839, Leader of the Sukerchakia **misl**, one of the Sikh armies, while still a boy. He managed to win the support of other Sikh groups and, by 1799, had captured Lahore. He was proclaimed Maharaja on Baisakhi 1801. He looked to the west to modernize his army and administration and ruled a kingdom which was secular in the Indian meaning of that word. All religions were respected but none was given a privileged position. One of his major achievements was the development of the town of Amritsar and with it the enhancement of the Darbar Sahib which he decorated with gold leaf so lavishly that it became known as the Golden Temple. After his death the British intervened and eventually annexed the Punjab in 1849.

Ravidās (*c.* 1414 – 1526, both dates are uncertain) Ravidas, also known as Rai Das was a chamar, a cobbler is how he described himself, an outcaste. He was a mystic of deep spirituality. Forty-one of his hymns are included in the Guru Granth Sahib.

In the late nineteenth century many chamars entered the Sikh Panth in the hope of improving their social status but without success. They responded from about 1907 onwards by setting up their own places of worship which are often similar in appearance to gurdwaras and have the Guru Granth Sahib as the focal point. However, to an increasing degree they use the word 'Sabha', association, rather than gurdwara, and while they may honour some of the Sikh Gurus, they pay special attention to celebrating the birthday of Guru Ravidas in February/March. The Ravidasis are now emerging as a distinct religious group, with shrines in Varanasi, where he was born, as well as in the Punjab.

Revelation Sikhism is to be regarded as a revealed religion, not a movement of social protest or an attempt to reconcile Hinduism and Islam through the creation of a synthesis which would appeal to both. It began with Guru Nanak's awareness of being taken to the divine court and commissioned to be God's messenger to the Kal Yug, the fourth cosmic age according to Hindu teaching, the one in which righteousness was forgotten, its characteristic being degeneracy. He asserted that he spoke only when God instructed him to do so and put the words into his mouth (AG 566). Each successive Guru was enlightened by the same source, each gave the same message, they differed from one another only in human form (AG 966). Sometimes portraits of the Gurus share considerable likenesses, the reason given being the unity of their teaching. In gurdwaras it is common to see portraits of only the first and last Gurus because all those coming between them gave the same message and therefore are represented in the other two.

Before he died Guru Gobind Singh asked to be taken into the presence of the Primal Guru. He was set in front of the **Adi Granth** which he now declared to be the Guru of the Sikhs. Nine years earlier he had instituted the **Khalsa**, stating that it was his other self. Thus Sikhs believe that the **Guru Granth Sahib** is the divine word, but also that the Panth is inspired to interpret it in each generation.

There is no concept of exclusive revelation in Sikh teachings. Other scriptures and teachers are to be respected as vehicles of revelation. The concept of an omnipresent, omnipotent God cannot allow them to believe other than that the True Being has been self-manifesting from the beginning of time. Witness is borne to this doctrine in the Adi Granth by the inclusion of the **bhagat bani**, compositions by non-Sikhs such as Ramanand, Kabir, and Sheikh Farid.

Ritual Guru Nanak opposed what he considered to be the ineffective and distracting rituals of Hinduism and Islam. Insistence of their careful observance resulted in a formalism which kept the worshipper preoccupied with the temporal to the

135

neglect of the spiritual. Thus he could assert that, 'Rituals and ceremonies are chains of the mind' (AG 635). He denounced them for encouraging the devotee to concentrate on them instead of God: 'Cursed be the ritual that makes us forget the Beloved' (AG 590).

His message was that men and women of all castes had direct access to God. They needed only to meditate upon the divine Name, Nam Simran. So he sould say, 'If they know the nature of God they will know rituals to be futile' (AG 470).

Sikhism has acquired its own rituals as have other movements which set out to achieve similar goals. It is part of the institutionalization process. However, there is no lack of preachers and writers who remind the Panth of the teachings of Guru Nanak and denounce ritualism, though often the concern is as much to prevent Hindu accretions as to reinforce the observance of **Nam Simran**.

Rumālā Literally a handkerchief, used of the cloths which are used as coverings for the Guru Granth Sahib. These are of two kinds, first those which are placed formally under and over the scripture, and secondly those given by devotees, frequently on important family occasions. Rumalas are also given by a sangat to men or women who are being honoured as part of a **saropa**.

Sabhā A Punjabi word for a society or association, used in a variety of contexts, the most famous being **Singh Sabha**.

Sach Khaṇḍ The Realm of Truth, the fifth and final stage of spiritual ascent. This is the abode of the Formless One where the believer enters into unity with God. Guru Nanak said, 'To describe it is as hard as steel' (AG 8). It can only be experienced not expressed in words. (See also **Heaven and Hell**.)

Sacrament If by the word sacrament the reference is to a means of grace then it must be said what is sometimes called the darshan of the word is the primary source for Sikhs. Darshan is what the devotee receives from seeing a guru in the Hindu tradition, a benign, grace bestowing, glance. In Sikhism it should be more than seeing the Guru Granth Sahib, it includes hearing the words, and being absorbed in the message. Both nam simran, private meditation, and diwan, congregational worship, may be regarded as sacramental in this sense. If the word is a translation of 'sanskar' there are four in Sikhism, naming, marriage, the ceremonies surrounding death, and initiation. These are considered to be rites of passage, not means of conferring or acquiring spiritual gifts or blessings. The word sacrament is probably inappropriate in the Sikh context.

Sāddhū A Hindu holy man, literally, 'one who is straight'. He has usually renounced the world and is celibate. For these reasons he does not stand high in the respect of Sikhs, no matter how virtuous and spiritual he might be, because of their emphasis upon the householder, **grihastha** life-style. Guru Amar Das argued, 'Family life is superior to the detached life, because it is from householders that ascetics meet their needs [i.e. by begging]' (AG 587).

Sadhna A butcher who lived in the thirteenth century and came from Sind. One of his hymns is included in the Adi Granth, on page 858.

Saguṇa With qualities. Used by Guru Nanak to assert that God becomes manifest as creator and Guru whilst denying belief in avatars. (See also **nirguṇa**.)

Sahaj The state of ultimate equipoise, spiritual peace, or bliss, resulting from the attainment of mystical union with God. Many terms are used of a person who has achieved sahaj, among the most used are gurmukh, one who is God-centred, braham-gyani, one who knows God, and jivan-mukt, one who is liberated while in the human body. Guru Tegh Bahadur described such a Sikh in these words: 'One to whom pleasure and pain are alike, and so too pride and shame; one who transcends joy and sorrow, and knows that is truly real; one who gives up both praise and slander and craves for the state of desirelessness' (AG 219).

Sahajdhāri Someone who has not received initiation into the Khalsa and does not follow the complete Sikh code of discipline. Literally a 'slow adopter' but nowadays much more often used in contrast to amritdhari, one who has been initiated, or kesdhari, one who keeps the outward Sikh form, especially uncut hair and the turban.

Sāhib Term of respect to one who is acknowledged to be a person's social superior. Thus in pre-independence India the British were often spoken of as 'sahibs'. It is used by Sikhs as a suffix to their scripture, the Guru Granth Sahib, and to certain places of historical significance, for example, the Darbar Sahib at Amritsar, or the town of Anadpur Sahib, where the Khalsa was instituted.

Saiṇ One of the bhagats who is said to have been a disciple of **Ramanand** and to have lived at the end of the fourteenth and beginning of the fifteenth century. He was a barber at the court of Raja Ram, king of Rewa. There is one of his hymns in the Adi Granth, on page 695.

Sākhī The literal meaning is 'testimony', thus the janam sakhis are testimonies to the lives of particular Gurus. Sakhi is used to refer to a section of a janam sakhi but sometimes also in a more general sense of 'story'.

Salutations The normal way for one Sikh to greet another is to place the hands together, bow slightly, and say 'Sat sri akal' frequently adding 'ji' as a mark of friendship which reduces the element of formality. The words mean, 'Truth is eternal'. When addressing the sangat in a gurdwara it is customary to begin and often end with the words, 'Wahiguruji ka Khalsa, wahegurji ki fateh', 'The Khalsa are the chosen of God, Victory be to God.' Sometimes the person who has spoken will be greeted by a member of the sangat shouting, 'Jo bole so nihal', to which other Sikhs will add 'Sat sri akal'. The precise meaning of the first part of this acclamation is uncertain, renderings usually convey the sense, 'Let everyone who is saved say . . . Truth is eternal'.

Salwār kameez (kamīz) Female dress popular in the Punjab, which consists of trousers (salwar) and long blouse (kamiz). Its wear is not confined to Sikhs and many Sikh women, especially in towns or outside India, dress in saris.

Sampradāya A religious tradition, school or sect. Sometimes also used of the teachings of the group.

Saṃsāra Literally 'going through'; the succession of transmigrations that the soul (atman) must pass through in its journey to final liberation. 'Coming and going' which is the most popular phrase used by the Gurus for the concept of transmigration, is the result of egoism, **haumai**, but the process only comes to an end by the will, **hukam**, of God. Sikhism has no place for a mechanistic operation of the law of **karma** which excludes divine initiative.

Samvat Sometimes also written 'sammat', it means a year. However, it is also used extensively in north India to indicate the dating system attributed to a King Vikramaditya, which commenced in 58 B.C.E. According to this system Guru Nanak was born in Samvat 1526, the dating used in the janam sakhis. Occasionally Samvat, abbreviated to 'S' is still used by Sikhs. 'Vikrami', or 'Bikrami' (Punjabi) may also be found. They may be abbreviated to Vk. or Bk..

Saṅgat A company or association, especially the congregation of a gurdwara or the local Sikh community. Often the word 'sadhsangat' or 'satsangat' is used, notably in the Guru Granth

139

Sahib. 'Holy congregation' of 'society of the saints' are commonly-found translations of it.

Sikhism is a religion which attaches considerable importance to community; there is no such thing as an ascetic Sikh who has decided to forsake the sangat in pursuit of personal salvation. The Gurus frequently spoke of their dependence upon the Sangat, and Guru Gobind Singh described the Khalsa as his other self. Guru Ram Das went so far as to say, 'Just as the wretched castor oil plant inbibes the scent of nearby sandalwood, so the fallen are emancipated by the association of the company of the saints' (AG 861).

In answer to the question 'Of what kind is the society of the saints?' Guru Nanak replied, 'The kind where only God's name is uttered' (AG 72), so indicating the primary purpose of the sangat. However, he also stated that those who sought 'a seat in God's court, should dedicate themselves to the service of people in this world' (AG 26).

Saṅgatia The person appointed by and responsible to Guru Amar Das to oversee one of the twenty-two groups into which he organized the Panth. From the time of Guru Arjan they came to be known as **masands**.

Saṅgrāṅd The time when the sun passes from one sign of the zodiac into another. It is observed with special services for worship by some Sikhs, presumably because of Hindu influence, even though the Gurus discounted the notion of one day being better or worse than another. As Guru Nanak said, 'In the process of calculating and fixing auspcious days, we forget that God is above such considerations' (AG 904).

Sannyās Renunciation. The fourth stage of life for a higher caste (twice-born) Hindu, but one which a brahmin may enter at any time. One who has taken sannyas is known as a sannyasin. Sikhism does not recognize it and pays no particular respect to those who have adopted the renunciate life. At worst the Gurus could consider them to be parasites, at best victims of self-deception; 'The ascetic's staff, the begging bowl, hair tuft, sacred thread, loin cloth, pilgrimage to holy places, wandering from place to place homeless, none of these brings peace. He who utters the Lord's Name swims across [the ocean of rebirth and death]' (Guru Nanak, AG 1127).

Sannyāsīn A man who has entered upon the fourth stage of life according to the Hindu tradition. Sikhism rejects both the practice of asceticism and the idea of progressive life stages, regarding the married state of the householder as the norm. Guru Nanak taught, 'He alone is a sannyasin who serves God and rids himself of conceit. He neither chatters nor talks in vain. He treasures forbearance and subdues his anger through God's name' (AG 1013).

Guru Gobind Singh advised Sikhs that their homes should be like forest retreats where they could live as sannyasins in their hearts.

Sansār Punjabi form of 'samsara' (Sanskrit), the cycle of birth and death.

Sanskāras The life-cycle rituals. For Sikhs these consist of naming, marriage, death, and initiation into the Khalsa.

Sant In the history of Indian religion the word sant is used to describe a group of teachers who flourished in the fifteenth, sixteenth, and seventeenth centuries in the northern part of the country. Though they had many things in common so that sometimes the term 'sant tradition' or 'sant sampradaya' is employed as an umbrella term of reference, there is no firm evidence for concluding that they knew one another or each other's teachings and compositions. The link between some of them and Ramanand would appear to be a response to criticisms that as non-brahmins their message could not be authentic. To trace it back to an eminent brahmin of the devotional form of Hinduism known as bhakti was a convenient solution.

The sants emphasized monotheism and devotion to God, but not through divine incarnations, avatars, which they tended to reject. They often employed the terminology of vaishnava bhakti as well as nath yoga, however, and sometimes the influence of Sufi Islam may be detected. They expressed their teachings in the form of bhajans, hymns, written in the language of the people. They rejected not only the use of Sankrit but also the claims of the brahmins to be the sole religious functionaries, and were frequently critical of ritualism, caste, and concepts of purity and pollution, all of which the brahmins endorsed. They were usually men of low caste. Among these sants were Namdev, Ravidas, and Kabir, each of whom is represented in the Guru Granth Sahib.

Sant is also used of individual Sikh preceptors who acquire reputations as teachers and spiritual guides. They do not, of course, claim to be gurus, only to be exponents of the teachings of the Sikh Gurus, but the respect they are given and the influence they wield is often similar to that accorded Hindu gurus. The prefix 'sant' will be placed before their name, for example, Sant Fateh Singh, but is only an honorific title bestowed by devotees and has no official status.

Sarbat Khālsā The literal meaning is 'all the Khalsa'. It is representative meeting of all Sikh parties and groups convened by the **jathedar** of the Akal Takht to consider important matters relating to the Panth. The tradition goes back to the misl period of the eighteenth century. Its underlying theology is that of the Guru Panth. (See **Gurū**.)

Sardār The equivalent to the English term 'Mr', though it carries with it a more respectful connotation as it actually means 'chief'. Sardarji is a word commonly used by an Indian who might be asking directions from a person he did not know but who had the outward appearance of a Sikh. Sometimes used instead of the word 'Sikh', e.g. 'our doctor is a sardar'.

Sardārni The female form of sardar, but less frequently used other than a direct term of address.

Saropā A robe of honour presented by the community to one of its own members or anyone else to whom it wishes to display formal respect. It often takes the form of a length of cloth for a turban, or a broad scarf to be worn over the shoulders (chuni).

Sarovar The pool for bathing which often forms part of a gurdwara complex.

Sat Gurū The supreme Guru, God. Other names are given to God in the Sikh tradition, most notably, Parmeshar, **Akal Purukh, Kartar Purukh**, and in popular usage, **Wahiguru**. However, Sat Guru is used three hundred times by Guru Nanak in the Adi Granth. For him God was his only Guru, and by using the word he may have been contrasting God, as the reliable, trustworthy, true Guru with false human gurus, or simply making use of a term popular among teachers like himself. In Sikhism it serves as a reminder that the way in which God becomes manifest is through the word, or **shabad**, that is the utterances of the Gurus and other inspired teachers.

Satī The practice of immolating a widow on the funeral pyre of her husband. It was severely denounced by the Sikh Gurus, especially Amar Das, perhaps because by now the Panth was expanding rapidly and there was a need to provide moral guidance on a number of areas where Sikh and Hindu values differed. He taught: 'She is not a sati who burns herself on the pyre of her spouse, Nanak; a sati is one who dies at the very shock of separation. A sati is one who lives in a state of contentment and adorns herself with good conduct, who serves and cherishes her Lord for ever and with all her heart' (AG 787).

Satsang Sometimes written 'sadhsangat' it is basically synonymous with the word 'sangat' meaning congregation or local community. However, in very early Sikh writings, for example the hymns of the Gurus, it is used in the way in which the word Panth is now used, that is to refer to the Sikh community as a whole.

143

Sat Sri Akāl The form of Sikh salutation or greeting. It means, 'Truth is eternal'.

Sattā and **Baiwaṇṭ** Two bards at the court of Guru Arjan who are usually mentioned together. Eight of their hymns were included in the Adi Granth and can be found on pages 966 – 968.

Sau Sākhīs A collection of instructions to the Sikh community purporting to come from Guru Gobind Singh but probably mid-nineteenth century in origin. The words might be loosely translated as 'The Hundred Sayings'. In Punjabi the rendering of the plural form would be 'sakhian' so Sau Sakhian may sometimes be found.

Scripture The most important scripture is the **Guru Granth Sahib** or Adi Granth which must be present at any act or worship and many other events in the life of the community, for example the solemnization of a marriage. The **Dasam Granth** may also be used but does not enjoy the same ceremonial status, is not regarded as Guru, and is not installed in gurdwaras. The works of Bhai Nand Lal and Bhai Gurdas may be read in gurdwaras to explain the teachings contained in the Guru Granth Sahib, but these occupy a lower position in the scriptural hierarchy than the other two books.

Seli The woollen cord which Guru Nanak wore around his turban and which was passed on to his successors until Guru Hargobind set it aside considering it no longer to be appropriate for a Sikh Guru to wear it. Among Muslim mystics, Sufis, the seli was worn to signify renunciation. Guru Nanak, a married man, wore it to indicate his belief that a Sikh should live in the world, but not in a worldly manner.

Sevā Service, known as seva or sewa, is an essential part of the life of every Sikh. It may take the form of work in the gurdwara, such as preparing or serving food, or looking after the shoes of worshippers, or it can entail serving the community at large by building a dispensary or school, hospital visiting, caring for victims of natural disasters or wars. The Gurus set an example by performing menial tasks and the emphasis is often upon manual work rather than making financial donations. These are known as 'dan', charity.

Guru Nanak taught that, 'A place in God's Court can only be attained if we do service to others in this world' (AG 26). He also said, 'Wandering ascetics, warriors, celibates, sannyasins, none of them obtains the fruit (i.e. liberation), without performing seva' (AG 992).

Sevā panthi A Sikh whose life is devoted to the service of the Sikh community. Also an organization of selfless workers established in honour of Bhai Kanayha, a Sikh who cared for the wounded on the battlefield regardless of whether they were friend or foe and was commended by Guru Gobind Singh for doing so.

Shabad (śabad) It has two related meanings: the first is the Word of God revealed to those whose compositions are contained in the Sikh scriptures; secondly, it is used to describe the hymns themselves.

Shaheed A martyr; a title placed before the name of someone who has died for the Sikh faith.

Shlok (shalok, ślok) Couplet found in the Guru Granth Sahib.

Shromaṇi Gurdwārā Parbandhak Committee (S.G.P.C.) In 1920 this body was established to be responsible for the organization of gurdwaras in Punjab and was given that duty under the Gurdwaras Act of 1925. With the passing of time it has extended the range of its influence to include such things as publishing and seeking to be accepted as the voice of Sikhism. One of its main concerns is education. It is responsible for the administration and funding of a number of schools and colleges, not all of them in the Punjab, and for the Guru Ram Das hospital in Amritsar. Politically it supports the Akali party whose members form the majority group in the committee. It has 175 members who are elected every five years.

Shuddhī sabhā   A purifying gathering used by Sikhs to counter the 'shuddhi' ceremonies of the Hindu Arya Samaj reform movement in the late nineteenth and early twentieth centuries. The Arya Samaj used these occasions to convert outcastes, Muslims, Sikhs and others to Hinduism. Shuddi sabhas were used to initiate members of other religious groups into the Sikh fold.

Siddha   One of the eighty-four perfected beings believed by the followers of **Gorakhnath** to have achieved immortality and to be living in the Himalayas. In the Sikh writings the terms siddha and **nath** are frequently used indiscriminately.

Siddha Gosht (Goṣṭ)   One of the most important of Guru Nanak's hymns, composed in the form of a discussion (gosht) with the **siddhas**. It is to be found between pages 937 and 943 of the Adi Granth. In it the Guru criticizes the approach to spirituality and the techniques of the **nath** yogis while at the same time providing an apologia for the new Sikh path to liberation based on the community of people following the householder way of life, honest labour, and **nam simran**. It also vindicates Guru Nanak's mission.

Sidharan path   A 'broken', or non-continuous reading of the Guru Granth Sahib, which takes place over a period of time, often nine days after a funeral. Used as the opposite to a continuous reading, **akhand path**.

Sikh   The word Sikh is derived from a Punjabi word meaning learner. Sometimes, therefore, it is translated as disciple. The issue of more precise definition is one which has frequently exercised the community, especially in the twentieth century. The

146

Rahit Maryada defines a Sikh as 'any person who believes in God; in the ten Gurus; in the Guru Granth Sahib and other writings of the Gurus, and their teaching; in the Khalsa initiation ceremony; and who does not believe in the doctrinal system of any other religion.' Attempts have been made from time to time to be even more rigorous. The Delhi Gurdwara Act of 1971 states that for the purpose of voting for the Delhi S.G.P.C. only those who have been initiated into the Khalsa are deemed to be Sikhs. The British Army recognized as Sikhs those soldiers who wore the turban and kept the hair uncut. After joining the army every Sikh had to be **amritdhari**.

Sikh Dharma of the Western Hemisphere The name recently adopted by the American Sikhs who converted to the religion as the result of the work of Yogi Harbhajan Singh, also known as the **Three HO movement**.

Sikh dispersion Most Sikhs are of Punjabi origin and of these, (estimates vary from thirteen to sixteen million), the vast majority live in the Punjab. There are two main explanations for this other than the obvious fact that this is where Sikhism began. First, the Sikh religion is not a missionary faith nowadays. Secondly, there is a strong attachment to the Punjabi language and culture. This strengthens the cohesion of the community but also presents would-be converts with an initial barrier. Consequently, the Sikhs one meets in Germany, Thailand, or Dubai, are likely still to have relatives in the Punjab even though they themselves may never have been there. Sikhs moved out of the geographical area of the Punjab not long after its annexation by the British in 1849. As members of the British Army they served in places like Hong Kong and later fought in the first world war. Before this, in the eighteen nineties, some civilians were recruited to work in East Africa, where some still remain, though after the British colonies in Africa became independent many Sikhs left for Britain, the U.S.A. or Commonwealth countries. Those who came to Britain joined Sikhs who had arrived there in the nineteen fifties and

147

sixties. British Sikhs now number over 300,000, the largest group outside India itself.

The principal reason for Sikh migration has been economic and the main areas chosen for settlement have been those which were part of the British Empire and other countries having English as their national language, though recently there has been a tendency to seek opportunities in continental Europe, but numbers are still small.

Few countries ask questions of religious affiliation in censuses so accurate numbers of Sikhs are difficult to calculate.

Sikhī Discipleship. The term is often used to refer to Sikh teachings understood in the broadest sense, as opposed to the Khalsa code prescribed in the **Rahit Maryada**.

Sikh language Punjabi provides the key to studying Sikhism and participating fully in the life of most Sikh communities because Sikhs are seldom more than three generations apart from the Punjab and the majority of migrants still speak Punjabi in their homes. The language of the Guru Granth Sahib has influenced Punjabi so that the two are almost regarded as synonymous, though actually they are not. The scripture is written in gurmukhi which is the script used by Sikhs in writing Punjabi (Muslims in Pakistan and India are likely to use the Urdu script to write Punjabi), and worship in the gurdwara is in Punjabi. The crisis in the Punjab during the nineteen eighties strengthened a movement going back about a hundred years to define Sikhism in terms of Punjabi language and culture. The growth of a third generation in countries such as the U.S.A., Canada, and Britain, who have little or no Punjabi is going to pose a problem for communities, but Punjabi is likely to retain a special place in Sikh worship for many years to come even in these countries.

Sikh reform movements There must always be creative tensions within any dynamic organism and the Sikh religion is no exception in this respect, though there is a natural anxiety to

148

regard movements which claim to be reformist in intention as threatening to undermine panthic cohesion and unity. The principal avowed aims of Sikh reform movements have been to purge it of Hindu influences and protect it from Hindu, especially Arya Samaj, and Christian missionary threats. Most notable have been the **Nirankari, Namdhari,** and **Singh Sabba** movements. The work of the latter has been taken up by the **Akali** party and the **Shromani Gurdwara Parbandhak Committee.**

Siṅgh A term used to describe those who follow the Khalsa code of discipline, the **Rahit Maryada,** rather than **sikhi,** a broader interpretation of the Sikh faith.

'Singh' is also the name which all male members of the Khalsa, and many other uninitiated Sikhs, use instead of, or as well as their clan name, e.g. Harbans Singh, or Harbans Singh Shan. (See **Names.**)

Siṅgh Sabhā In 1834 the Ludhiana Mission was set up by American protestant Christians, Conversions, especially of young intellectuals, caused a degree of anxiety which eventually expressed itself in the Singh Sabha movement. The first association, which 'sabha' means, was formed in 1873 in Amritsar with Thakur Singh Sandwalia as president and Giana Gian Singh as secretary. In 1877 the Arya Samaj, a Hindu reform movement, also became active in the Punjab. At first they were regarded by the Sikhs as allies against the missionaries, but soon it was seen that they too formed a threat to the Panth. As a consequence Singh Sabhas proliferated. Their policy was to counter these opponents by developing schools and colleges of their own and by producing literature so that Sikhs might be as able to defend their faith as their enemies were to attack it. Many institutions known as Khalsa colleges owe their existence to the movement. Later, the reaction took on political dimensions and led to the formation of the **Akali** party, the agitation for Sikh control of gurdwaras, and the setting up of the **Shromani Gurdwara Parbandhak Committee.**

Smoking One of the strongest Sikh restrictions is on the use of tobacco in any form. It is listed as one of the four **kurahts** (probitions) in the Sikh Code of Discipline. An initiated Sikh who smokes must be reinitiated again for breaching the **rahit**. This is a regulation which the great majority of Sikhs take seriously. Visitors to gurdwaras should not even carry cigarettes with them and it is a courtesy not to smoke in a Sikh home.

Sodār see **Rahirās**.

Soḍhi The **khatri** subcaste or gotra to which the fourth and succeeding Gurus belonged.

Sohilā Kirtan Sohila is one of the most important hymns in the Guru Granth Sahib. It occurs twice, once in the collection of hymns intended for daily devotional use, (AG 12), and then on page 157. It contains three hymns by Guru Nanak, and one each by the fourth and fifth Gurus. They should be sung just before going to sleep and are also used at funerals.

Sri Chand (1492 – 1612) Eldest son of Guru Nanak, he was a person of deep spirituality but instead of following the path taught by his father he became an ascetic and the founder of an order known as **Udasis**.

Sukh asan The phrase means 'to sit comfortably'. It is the name given to the ceremony which takes place at the end of the day when the Guru Granth Sahib is formally closed for the night. The prayer **Ardas** is read, and a random reading taken from the book (**vak**), which is then closed and covered with **rumalas**. If it is taken from the throne (palki), where it has been throughout the day, it will be carried to its resting place on a Sikh's head. Worshippers on either side of it will bow, those behind it will form a procession. Many of the congregation will chant until the doors of the room where it has been put are closed. (See also **parkash karṇā**.)

Sukhmani sāhib This composition by Guru Arjan, found in the Adi Granth on pages 262 to 296, is one of the greatest and most respected in the Punjabi language. It is recited daily by Hindus as well as Sikhs as an aid to meditation. The theme of peace is stated in a couplet which occurs frequently as a refrain throughout the twnety-four sections. It runs: 'The Name of God is sweet ambrosia, source of inner peace and joy. The Name of God brings blissful peace to the hearts of the truly devout.'

The title means either Peace of Mind, or Pearl of Peace, depending upon whether 'mani' is to be understood as pearl or mind.

Sunder A grandson of Guru Amar Das represented in the Adi Granth by six hymns which are located on pages 923 and 924. ('Sundar' is also used.)

Surat shabad yoga A form of meditation discipline which aims at merging the soul with the sound of hymns, thus producing spiritual harmony.

Surdas A brahmin who governed the province of Sandila during the reign of Akbar the Great. He was born in 1528. One of his compositions is to be found in the Guru Granth Sahib, on page 1253.

Swayyā, savayyā A poetic form used in the Guru Granth Sahib. The term also refers to a group of panegyrics composed by the tenth Guru and contained in the Dasam Granth.

Takht A seat of temporal authority, literally, a throne. There are five gurdwaras which are designed as takhts. They are,

Akal Takht, Amritsar. This was established by Guru Hargobind in 1609 on a site opposite the Harmandir Sahib.

Patna Sahib, in Bihar,

Keshgarh, at Anandpur Sahib in the Punjab,

Nander near Hyderabad, Maharashtra,

Damdama Sahib, near Batinda in the Punjab. This was
declared to be a takht in 1966 by the Shromani Gurdwara
Parbandhak Committee.

By the time Guru Hargobind became leader of the Sikhs the
influence of the Guru had become temporal as well as spiritual.
The building of the Akal Takht facing the focus of spirituality, the
Darbar Sahib, was a way of recognizing and drawing attention to
the duality of function. Since 1609 it has been a place from which
important decisions relating to the life of the Panth have been
issued. The purpose of the takhts, spread as they are throughout
India, though in places associated with Guru Gobind Singh in
respect of three of them, is really to safeguard correctness of
practice but, perhaps inevitably, they have taken on political roles
and sometimes pronounced upon matters which could be
regarded as doctrinal. Such issues, however, are properly the
responsibility of the whole Panth which should assemble at a
meeting convened for the purpose, a Sarbat Khalsa.

The head of each Takht is called a jathedar and is appointed by
the S.G.P.C., which makes decisions. Appointments tend to be
for life. Sometimes the jathedar is described as a head priest. This
is an extremely unfortunate misnomer for not only is Sikhism a
totally lay religion with no priesthood, but also the jathedar is
chosen with administrative and sometimes political rather than
pastoral considerations in mind.

Tankhā When a Sikh has breached the disciplinary code of the
Khalsa, the Rahit Maryada, he or she should come to the local
sangat, confess the fault and accept punishment for the offence.
This will be determined by five members, the panj piare. The
penalty imposed will usually be of a light and menial nature, such
as fetching water for langar or for cleaning the gurdwara, or
wiping and polishing the dusty shoes of worshippers. It should
demonstrate the public repentance of the wrongdoer without
leaving a feeling of resentment or lasting humiliation. The
ultimate aim is the reinstatement of the offender into the sangat.
For very serious infringements of the rahit, known as **kurahts**,

152

reinitiation will be required at a time when the sangat considers that the person found guilty of indiscipline is thought to be ready to purge the contempt.

Tankha actually means 'salary' and is one of many uses of terms which in practice state the opposite to the intention.

Taruna Dal The army of the younger ones in contrast to the **Buddha Dal** in the eighteenth century. Part of the Sikh army known as the **Dal Khalsa**.

Tat Khālsā A thorough-going reform of Sikh conduct and discipline proposed by some members of the **Singh Sabha** movement at the beginning of the twentieth century. 'Tat' means hot and refers to the zeal with which they pursued their aims.

Teen Tap These are the three forms of suffering from which deliverance is asked in the formal Sikh prayer, Ardas. They are mental, bodily, and those which are psychological, such as doubt. God is seen to be the one who alone can remove these: 'The Lord's glory is spread everywhere. My ailments of mind (adi), body (biadi), and doubt (upadi), are eradicated. I am rid of the three fevers (teen tap)' (Guru Arjan AG 1223).

Tegh Bahādur, Gurū (born 1 April 1621, Guru 20 March 1665 to 11 November 1675.) The ninth Guru was the second son of Guru Hargobind but only became Guru himself after the death of his nephew and grand nephew, the seventh and eighth Gurus. Guruship was never hereditary in the sense of succession necessarily passing to the eldest son, but if an explanation is needed it may lie in the early nickname he was given, Degh Bahadur, brave cooking pot, because of his devotion to feeding the hungry. When the Mughal rulers were pursuing policies of Islamization it may have been felt that someone more politically motivated was needed to lead the Sikh movement. When the retiring Tyag Mal, to use his given name, became Guru he quickly responded to the situation so much so that he is now

153

known by a new name, Tegh Bahadur, brave sword. One hundred and sixteen of his compositions were placed in the Guru Granth Sahib by his son. To the extent of uttering the **gurbani**, Guru Tegh Bahadur returned to the early tradition of guruship, but he is more famous for his opposition to the Emperor Aurangzeb's attempts to impose Islam on his subjects. This eventually led to his arrest and death after he had refused the offer of keeping his life on condition that he became converted to the Islamic faith. He was executed in Delhi at the place where the gurdwara Sis Ganj now stands; his remains were smuggled out of the city by some devotees of the sweeper, chuhra, caste. His body was cremated on the site now occupied by gurdwara Rekab Ganj, also in Delhi, the head being taken to his son at Anandpur where it too was cremated.

Among Sikhs and Hindus the Guru is respected as a martyr in the cause of religious liberty. As Guru Gobind Singh, his son put it; 'He died to preserve their right to wear their caste marks and sacred thread; he suffered martyrdom for the sake of his faith' (Vichitar Natak).

Tenth Door This, the dasam dwar, is the mystical opening which, according to **hatha yoga** teaching, gives access to the condition of equipoise known as **sahaj**. The other nine doors are the natural orifices of the body.

Three HO In January 1959 Harbhajan Singh Puri began teaching yoga in the U.S.A. Some of the young men and women who attended his classes became interested in the whole life-style which he advocated and were converted to Sikhism. Yogi Bhajan, as he is known, encourages families to live together in ashrams where they can support one another in the practice of their faith. These American Sikhs are recognizable by their completely white dress which though Punjabi has a distinctiveness of style. Women as well as men wear the turban. Ram Das is the Guru to whom they attach particular respect, though of course all are seen to be equally enlightened. They are particularly scrupulous in observing the whole Code of Discipline, the Rahit. Some send their children to Sikh schools in India to receive at least part of their education. Yogi Bhajan's movement was known as the 3HO, the Healthy, Happy, and Holy Organization, but members seem to prefer to be known as American Sikhs, part of the world-wide Sikh community.

Tīrath   See **Pilgrimage**.

Trilochan   A Hindu bhagat of vaishya caste from the Bombay region. He lived in the late thirteenth century being born, it is said, in 1267. He is represented in the Adi Granth by four compositions on pages 92, 525, and 695.

Turban   This, probably the best known feature of Sikhism, is not one of the five Ks which a Khalsa Sikh must wear, though the Code of Discipline, **Rahit Maryada**, states that men must cover their heads with it but it is optional for women. All pictures of the Gurus show them with turbans but tradition asserts that their followers began to emulate them only in the time of Guru Gobind Singh. When his father was martyred there were no Sikhs brave enough to share his fate; all those present remained anonymous in the crowd. The young Guru commanded that henceforward such cowardice should not be permitted, a Sikh should be recognizable by his turban. It is also said that a reason for its being adopted was so that in fighting between Mughals and Sikhs innocent Hindus would be less likely to be harmed if the Sikhs could be easily identified.

Despite its association with Sikhism, the turban is not exclusive to Sikhs though their stylish and smart appearance tends to distinguish them. The colour of the turban is not significant but blue is sometimes worn by supporters of the Akali political party, orange may denote one who sympathizes with the campaign for an independent Punjab state, Khalistan, and Namdharis wear white turbans tied flat across the forehead. American converts, members of the 'Three HO' movement, both men and women, also have white turbans. Sikh members of the Congress party also wear white turbans.

Udāsī In the Sikh context this word has two very different meanings. First, it is used of the journeys of Guru Nanak during the two decades of his itinerant preaching ministry. Secondly, it refers to an order of ascetics begun by Baba Sri Chand, 1494 – 1612, the eldest son of Guru Nanak. Their centres known as akharas, are to be found in many places in north India. No link with the teachings or traditions of Sikhism now remain; on the contrary they appear to be part of mainstream Hinduism, the children in their schools learning Sanskrit, for example, and the temples having murtis of the principal Hindu deities.

Updeshak A preacher who exhorts, encourages and advises the faithful, teaching them how to become more observant Sikhs. Schools for training them was one of the features of the **Singh Sabha movement** through the **Chief Khalsa Diwan**.

Vaisakh An alternative form of the word **Baisakhi**

Vāk Vak laina, or the seeking of advice by opening the Guru Granth Sahib at random after prayerful deliberation is a long-established Sikh practice. The scripture is held in such a way that the spine of the book rests on a surface, then the hands supporting the covers are allowed to move slowly outwards so that the book may fall open at any page. The vak is then taken by reading the first line of the first complete hymn on the left-hand page.
  Part of the daily installation ceremony of the Guru Granth Sahib is taking a vak. In many gurdwaras this will then be written or typed and placed on a notice board so that anyone coming to the gurdwara in the course of the day may consult it and so receive the the Guru's advice. A vak is also taken at the end of worship, diwan, and on many other occasions. Before agreeing to hold discussions with Prime Minister Rajiv Gandhi, the late Sant

Harchand Singh Longowal took a vak and was told, 'Act courageously and stop being in two minds on vital questions' (*India Today*, 15 August 1985).

Vālmīki See **Bālmīki.**

Vār A var is an epic poem but in the Guru Granth it takes the form of a hymn in praise of the spiritual exploits of God. The most famous is Asa ki Var found between pages 462 and 475 of the Adi Granth. It is sung daily in major gurdwaras early in the morning.

Varna The name given to the fourfold division of Indian society, usually translated by the word 'caste' in English. (see also **Caste**.)

Varnāshramadharma (varnāśrama-dharma) The fourfold caste (varna) division of Hindu society with the four stages of life (dharmas) and aims of life (arthas) which twice-born Hindus should follow. The implicit teaching of Guru Nanak was that this should be rejected as a futile solution to the search for spiritual liberation. For him there was one humanity, one dharma, that of the married family person (gristhi in Punjabi), and one life goal, liberation (mukti), which could be pursued alongside the moderate accumulation of wealth, enjoyment of pleasure, and fulfilment of social obligations. This way of life was open to women as well as men.

Vegetarianism The Gurus were loath to pronounce upon such matters as the eating of meat or ways of disposing of the dead because undue emphasis on them could detract from the main thrust of their message which had to do with spiritual liberation. However, Guru Nanak did reject by implication the practice of vegetarianism related to ideas of pollution when he said, 'All food is pure; for God has provided it for our sustenance' (AG 472).

Many Sikhs are vegetarian and meat should never be served at langar. Those who do eat meat are unlikely to include beef in their diet, at least in India, because of their cultural proximity to Hindus.

Veil The practice of women veiling themselves is discouraged in the Sikh community not only because it is regarded as a Muslim custom, but also as it is thought to imply an attitude which is not in keeping with the egalitarian spirit of the religion. The Code of Discipline specifically states that 'It is contrary to Sikh belief for women to veil their faces'. However, there is still a tendency for Sikh females to pull the dupatta, the scarf which many of them wear on the shoulders, over the hair as a mark of respect or modesty when they meet men outside the family circle, or elderly men within it.

Vices The Sikh concept of God as the one ultimate reality and creator carries with it the belief that evil and vices must somehow come from God. The alternative would be to accept some sort of dualism which Sikh theology abhors. Human beings have within them both vices and virtues. Guru Nanak said, 'The mortal is brimful of vices, but virtues abide in him too. Without the Guru and so long as he does not reflect upon the Name, he does not perceive the virtue' (AG 936).

The number of vices is listed as five. Guru Amar Das stated, 'Within this body are hidden five thieves: they are lust, wrath, greed, attachment and egoism. They steal away the nectar within us, but we fail to realize it because of our ego and no one hears our complaint' (AG 600).

In Punjabi the names of the five vices are, kam, krodh, lobh, moh, and hankar. The meaning of the first three vices is straightforward enough to require little explanation. Inordinate sexual desire, anger and the unrestrained pursuit of worldly gain result in lack of self-discipline and the tendency to ignore or discount the possibility of a spiritual dimension to life. Attachment is more in need of examination, being perhaps unfamiliar to the western mind. It means clinging to anyone or thing which prevents someone from becoming united with the one being who can provide eternal union, sahaj, God. Thus Guru Nanak wrote, 'Abandon love of family and of all affairs. Leave aside love of the world, it is a waste of time. Forsake worldly love and superstition, brother, it is all a waste of time' (AG 356).

He uses the familiar Indian symbol of the lotus which can survive in a murky pond, its beauty unspoiled by the filth which surrounds it to illustrates the idea of non-attachment: 'As the lotus lives detached in water, as the duck floats carefree on the stream, so one crosses the sea of material existence with the mind attuned to the Word. Live detached, shorn of hope, living in the midst of hope' (AG 938).

Hankar is notoriously difficult to translate. Ego, pride, are used, but scholars cannot agree on a satisfactory rendering. Hankar is the result of haumai, a word creating equal and similar problems but having the implications of self-reliance rather than trust in God. Something of the meaning is perhaps conveyed through the following quotations from Guru Nanak: 'The real asses are those who are full of self-pride but actually have no virtue to be proud of.' (AG 1246). 'You cannot stay in this world permanently so why do you walk in it puffed up with hankar?' (AG 473).

Virtues Virtues as well as vices are part of the human potential but unlike the latter which are usually spoken of as being five, there is no limit upon the number of virtues. The most important in the teaching of the Gurus are the practice of truth ('The highest virtue of all is truth, but higher still is truthful living' AG 62), purity of body and mind, temperance, contentment, forgiveness, justice, and patience. All these are acquired only through meditation upon the Name (of God) for these are characteristics of God from whom the devotee derives them.

Waḍḍā Ghallūghārā (Vaḍā ghallūghārā) On 5 February 1762 the forces of the Afghan ruler, Shah Abdali, came upon a Sikh force together with large numbers of noncombatant women, children and old men, near a village called Kup between Lahore and Barnala. Estimates of the number killed vary from ten to thirty thousand. The original copy of the Guru Granth Sahib compiled by Guru Gobind Singh was lost in the battle. It has been said that almost a third of the population of Sikhs were killed or wounded in the incident which is known as the Wadda Ghallughara, the Great Holocaust. In 1746 a similar catastrophe had befallen a Sikh force north of Lahore; seven thousand died and the three thousand prisoners were executed at Shahidganj in Lahore. This is known as the Little Holocaust, Chota Ghallughara.

Wāhigurū (Vāhigurū) Wonderful Lord, Wahiguru is the popular name by which Sikhs refer to or name God. Literally it means 'Praise to the Guru!' The word does not occur in Guru Nanak's writings in the Guru Granth Sahib but is found in the janam sakhis, being used in nam simran meditation as it is still. The suggestion has been made that the name is derived from the initial letters of the Hindu deities who were worshipped in each of the different yugas or cosmic ages, Vasdev, Hari, Krishna, Ram, and Gobind, (Var 1 of Bhai Gurdas), slightly rearranged, but there is no need to look for such a complex etymology; 'Vah Guru', 'Praise the Guru' is a natural spontaneous utterance.

It is found on pages 1402 and 1404 of the Adi Granth in words of the bards (bhatts) of Guru Arjan's court: 'Our praiseworthy Wahigrur, Wahiguru, Wahiguru, you are eternally just and true, the abode of excellence, the Primal Person' (AG 1402).

Washing of Hands This is regarded as being of practical importance rather than ritual significance. After removing shoes on entering a gurdwara the Sikh will wash the hands to remove the dust or mud which may have become attached to them. This will also be done before handling the Guru Granth Sahib.

Widows The Gurus opposed the practice of sati, the immolation of a widow upon her husband's funeral pyre, and asserted that widows should be accorded the same respect as that given to any .

160

other person. They should also be allow to remarry. Such marriages are conducted according to full Sikh rites.

Woman One of the most famous verses in the Guru Granth Sahib is that of Guru Nanak which says; 'It is from woman the despised one that we are conceived, it is from her that we are born. It is to woman that we are engaged and married. It is woman who is our life-long companion, and who perpetuates the race. It is she who is sought after when a man becomes a widower. We establish our social ties through her. Why then condemn her from whom great men and kings are born?' (AG 473).

In Hindu society woman was a prime cause of ritual pollution; in India mythology she was often a fickle temptress. Guru Nanak, however, recognized that if all life emanated from the one source, God, there could be no divinely created divisions of race, class, or sex. He therefore denounced Hindu and Muslim attitudes to women if they seemed to threaten their status as full human beings. This position was sustained by later Gurus in their condemnation of female infanticide, the practice of immolating widows on the funeral pyres of their husbands, or the giving of dowries to secure the marriage of a daughter. In positive respects too there was an endorsement of the principle of equality. Women served as missionaries, **peerhas**, the remarriage of widows was accepted, and, at the initiation ceremony at Baisakhi 1699 Mata Sahib Kaur helped prepare the amrit, something unthinkable in Brahminical Hinduism. In contemporary Sikhism there are no aspects of the religion in which a woman may not participate fully, including those of serving as a granthi or being one of the panj piare at ceremonies in which they participate. Any obstacles facing women within Sikhism are not of a theological nature but have to do with traditional attitudes to them in Indian Society. The modesty which society requires of them, especially in dress, is part of an injunction which should apply equally to men and women not to 'wear clothes which cause pain to the body or breed evil in the mind' (AG 16).

Yoga The practice of yoga as an aid to meditation, nam simran, is considered perfectly acceptable. However, Guru Nanak was wary of its practitioners, especially the Nath or Kanphata yogis, because of their claims to possess occult powers and the attempts they made to exploit credulous villagers. He also disagreed with their life-style which put the emphasis upon celibacy, asceticism, and renunication in general. On the other hand, he believed that God could, and should be found through the householder, gristhi, way of life and direct spiritual experience in the attainment of which rituals played no part. He denounced such yogic practices many times in passages like the following: 'The Ascetic's staff, the begging bowl, hair tuft, sacred thread, pilgrimages to holy places, wandering homeless from place to place, none of these bring peace. Peace is not obtained without the Lord's Name (i.e. nam simran). He who utters the Lord's Name swims across.' (AG 1127). 'The way of the true yogi is found by dwelling in God and remaining detached in the midst of worldly attachments' (AG 730).

Yugas The Gurus accepted the Hindu cyclical concept of time and with it the belief in four eras or kalpas or ages (yugas). However, they also rejected the idea of auspicious or inauspicious times and one feels that they referred to the four yugas only for convenience. What mattered to them was not that the present, fourth age, the kal yug, began on 17/18 February 3102 B.C.E. (Gregorian calendar dating), but that men and women need to know God in order to pass from this earthly existence into the sphere of life with Akal Purukh, the One who is Beyond Time. Nevertheless, many Sikhs will speak of Guru Nanak as God's messenger to the kal yug, sent to summon people to the true practice of religion, devotion to God's Name, at a time when it had been forgotten and replaced by ritualism, and righteousness had given way to oppression.

Zafarnāmā A letter, written in Persian, addressed to the Emperor Aurangzeb by Guru Gobind Singh in which he defiantly

162

denounced him as a tyrant and laid down the Sikh doctrine of resistance to oppression by physical force: 'When all avenues have been explored, all means tried, it is rightful to draw the sword from the scabbard and wield it with your hand.' It is contained in the **Dasam Granth**.

Zāt Punjabi form of the word 'jati', an endogamous caste grouping.